PROFESSIONALISM ON THE PAGE

To John,
Thankyou for your
interest.

PROFESSIONALISM ON THE PAGE

Mind, Method and Misadventure
with Words at Work

By Barry C. Scott

BROWN
DOG
BOOKS

Published under licence by Brown Dog Books and
The Self-Publishing Partnership, 7 Green Park Station, Bath BA1 1JB

www.selfpublishingpartnership.co.uk

Printed book ISBN: 978-1-78545-150-8
e-book ISBN: 978-1-78545-151-5

Cover design by Kevin Rylands
Internal design by Andrew Easton

Printed and bound by CPI Group (UK) Ltd,
Croydon CR0 4YY

ABOUT THE AUTHOR

Barry C. Scott is an expert in dealing with the cogency and readability of the written work produced by a wide spectrum of professional people. He has extensive and specialist professional writing experience gained from challenging circumstances, having written hundreds of documents for public consumption and unearthed shortcomings in the written work of others in thousands of cases.

In the last 10 years of his career, he acted in the prestigious role of a Consultant Planning Inspector on behalf of the Government, being personally responsible for all manner of development appeal decisions. Before that, he held a long-term senior management position in Local Government, being responsible for maintaining teams of professional workers and especially the calibre of their written work. He is an honours graduate and a Chartered Town Planner by training.

DEDICATION

To all members of my extended family. May you each come to appreciate the value in finding the best in yourselves and seeing the good in others, knowing the essence of fruitful communication.

AUTHOR'S NOTE

I have written this book because I know how poor the writing of so-called professional people can be, which sadly is the case much too often. Evidently, the many available grammar and style guides miss the point, which is that writing reflects mental acuity; it exposes your intellect on the page, where you are expected to show your above average abilities, for which you have (or will have) recognition. That is where the source of accomplished performance lies and it is my take on the matter, which distinguishes this book from the rest.

My book you will cause you to think carefully as much about your words as you do your subject. Through awareness and responsibility it will prime you not to disappoint, to face-up to potential misadventures in professional writing and do better.

ACKNOWLEDGEMENTS

As I have written from experience, rarely has the need presented itself to cite the published work of others. I list at the end of the book the works I do cite, alongside some other titles that have helped me clarify or confirm my own experience and understanding.

I am generally indebted to my former peers at the Government's Planning Inspectorate, from whom I obtained much enlightenment, more than at any other stage in my career.

The support, encouragement and forbearance of my wife have been priceless in my ambition to share my experience in this way.

Barry C. Scott BA (Hons) MRTPI (Rtd.)

TABLE OF CONTENTS

PREFACE

The appeal of this book

Professionalism on the Page is for the professionally intent person in any one of dozens of white-collar occupations. It is directed particularly at those in, or embarking upon, career occupations in the service and allied professions. These occupations render a service to a client directly or indirectly through individual, team or bureaucratic endeavour, and chiefly through mental acuity.

Above all, it is where a written product is central to professional performance. *Professionalism on the Page*, therefore, is relevant to the many disciplines and businesses where literary performance establishes in the mind of the customer/client the credentials of not just the person, but also the organisation they represent.

Professionalism on the Page will appeal to all those who wish to perform fully as professional people because it offers insight and experience that no amount of training in professional writing can touch.

It will open the eyes of the great many in professional life who are either uncomfortable with or blissfully unaware of their level of expertise when it comes to communicating it in writing. With the benefit of the insight and experience herein, these people will come to see the value of an approach that positively connects mental acuity with literary skill.

What this book is about

This book is about being truly professional. It is about character – of the person and of the language that expresses it. As will become clear, the character of language punishes those whose professionalism is suspect, where thinking is blinkered.

Professionals greatly rely upon written language as an instrument of their work, yet give it little thought. That is unfortunate because much goes wrong between thought and deed, irrespective of grammatical proficiency and formal training. Indeed, many business organisations steadfastly put improvement in written communication in the top ten wish list for better performance, above the likes of problem-solving and creative thinking.

The character of written English is a wondrous but perilous thing. Take this simple example adapted from a children's tongue-twister:

A racehorse named 'one' has a record of winning once; another named 'one-two' has a record of winning twice.

Now try this version of equal length:

'One' was a racehorse. 'One-two' was one, too. When 'one' won one race, 'one-two' won one, too.

Playing with language shows the potential for misadventure between thought and deed, when accuracy, precision and clarity are compromised (for the record, in the confusion of the second version the reader is unaware of how many races 'one-two' was successful in).

Into that cauldron of misadventure plunge the effects of the misconception that it is helpful to write as we speak. Then enters the awkward realisation that the English language is fed by changing needs, with its own momentum of often controversial innovation and initial usage that then has the chance to become established in the Oxford English Dictionary by popular demand. That there is no overall control and management of English is the crux of the matter. By contrast, consider French, which has the institution of the Academie Francaise, founded in 1634, as well as the General Commission on Terminology and Neology that seek to protect the language. It is no wonder that when English has unbridled freedom, meaning will undoubtedly become confused or lost through thoughtlessness.

Written work, as the instrument of professional endeavour, relates to notes, reports, statements and the like. It conveys a message of expertise derived from advanced education and/or training, amplified by beneficial experience. Readers will demand that the choice and arrangement of words exemplify the drive the professional person has in doing the right thing and doing it well in the face of difficult circumstances, taking pride in the result.

Difficulties impinge upon the writing task in all sorts of ways, not least because of the complexities of both the subject matter and the work environment. Those who fail to confront such difficulties and who trust in thoughtless habitual performance are consigned to the consequences of misadventure. Command of a professional writing style, correct 'Standard' English as deemed to be, including the acceptable departures established from common usage, and indeed 'official' English, is no more than a comfort blanket if inadequate thought lies beneath.

Professionalism on the Page is about slovenly writing that comes to grief through misadventure with the perils of English through thoughtlessness. It examines the common weaknesses and failings in fault-laden written work by reference to professional awareness and responsibility. From attitudes to actions, it shows the way to overcome thoughtlessness. Through raising professional awareness and responsibility in response to particular concerns about conduct, *Professionalism on the Page* connects mental acuity with literary skill, which is its main theme.

What this book offers

This is a 'how not to' book: that is, how not to engage in misadventure and fall victim to the unexpected hazards of the pitfalls and minefield that imperil the writing task. What happens to the witless victim and how not to be one orientate the professional person to write accurately, precisely and clearly.

Professionalism on the Page formulates codes of awareness and responsibility to guide the professionally intent person past the pitfalls and minefield that threaten performance. The codes demonstrate how attitudes bear down on mental acuity and show what it takes to gain full, positive control of the writing task. Root causes to potentially fault-laden written work are vividly exposed to be held at bay.

The codes exhort a professional character with which a thinking discipline is presented, orientated by a realistic method for true professional endeavour. *Professionalism on the Page* offers accomplishment beyond correctness with words.

Professionalism on the Page awakens a vital professional interest in working with words, connecting thought with deed for accomplished performance. It distinctively brings a comprehensive approach to self-learning and training, dealing with all aspects of professional conduct. The content is drawn from experience over a professional lifetime and is presented in a vivid and practical way.

INTRODUCTION

*The key to all knowledge is to be found in words
of one syllable.*

Anon

It was Einstein who commented to the effect that you should be capable of explaining your work to an eight-year-old in just one sentence. That sentence would be accurate, precise and clear, qualities that would move workplace writing towards the Holy Grail of manageable brevity, for the writer and reader both.

English is a rich language and there is always a way to say exactly what you mean, but it does require organised thought. As long ago as 1948, Sir Ernest Gowers (of 'Plain Words' renown) remarked about the difficulty of writing what you mean and influencing your readers as you intend. He commented that very few could do this on a first attempt and that few common things are more difficult than finding the right words.

With accomplished, thoughtful choice and arrangement of words, a writer comprehensively expresses something correctly and truthfully for readers confidently to take as accurate. Applying a relevant sharp focus, as against a broad light, readers see it in a precise context. Setting it down concisely without mystery and ambiguity, readers appreciate the clarity of meaning which stands out, and are not overwhelmed. That is what professional people are trusted to do in their everyday work. Very high, exacting standards are called for, which is no easy task.

Take this actual, somewhat intricate example:

Now that a Wordsworth revival seems to be at hand, interest in the poet will naturally increase.

This, in fact, is thoughtless writing, being devoid of accuracy, precision and clarity. Firstly, if a revival only 'seems' to be at hand, how can it be true that interest will 'naturally' increase; if there is doubt in the former, then there must be doubt in the latter. The sentence is thereby inaccurate. Secondly, does the writer use the phrase 'the poet' generically to refer to another or others, or to refer again to Wordsworth; if the latter, the writer should write 'him'. The sentence is thereby imprecise. Finally, readers are left with no clarity of the meaning intended by the writer, for the sentence is somewhat pointless or, at best, an elaborate duplication.

Countless present-day offerings in the body of experience behind *Professionalism on the Page* point to a lack of accomplishment, because of recurring difficulties of one kind or another. When troubled by difficulties, misadventure takes hold and faulted written work is mired where manageable brevity has no foothold, where accuracy, precision and clarity elude the writer. Much less than 10% of thousands of written submissions have impressed this author, irrespective of the levels of seniority, from students to managers alike.

What is going on in the writer's mind is crucial to understanding what often goes wrong on the page. Poor writing is associated with poor thinking and vice versa. Poor thinking is regularly a casualty of poor attitude. Much greater thoughtfulness towards written work is necessary, and the relevance and importance of this book are in demonstrating why and how to give it.

The written material of professional people is in the form of conventional documents or electronic transmissions where words are the 'tools of the trade' and a pragmatic text of workmanlike, official or utilitarian quality is produced. Writing performance typically rests on whatever initial training takes place, especially when attending a university. Essays and assignments are encouraged to adhere to the declared skills of a professional writing style, which itself may not be explicitly taught. Thereafter, it is down to the gaining of experience in the workplace by following the best examples offered and those that come to hand, occasionally augmented by self-learning or other training opportunities.

There is no denying that beneficial experience is indispensable – indeed, this book relies upon it. General experience, however, does not guarantee fully competent performance to exacting standards unless there is good fortune and a positive outlook. Even so, these are shaky foundations if unassisted by other means. All too easily, slovenly performance through sloppy thinking, careless application and cloudy complication occurs and a thoroughly befuddled written product ensues.

Good fortune in the workplace is often a haphazard occurrence and being able to capitalise upon it is an uncertain and prolonged affair. Instructive experience tends to be metered out over many years in the shape of chance encounters with numerous, diverse and demanding situations. Competence then emerges realistically, if at all, late in life. Not all professionally intent people profit from such situations, primarily because a positive outlook becomes a casualty of potentially hostile and difficult working environments.

Many professional people work within organisations. The typical, day-to-day practice of not having written work passed by senior colleagues, unless suggested amendments are favourably considered for incorporation, is often a capricious way of obtaining instructive experience. Suggested amendments may not be particularly helpful, especially if they are the product of questionable motives or perfunctory attention.

Such 'red-penning' may be due to personal preferences or, at best, to those supervisors and senior managers expediently ensuring that certain contextual requirements of the particular organisation are met, concerning style, legibility, emphasis, coverage etc. Seldom is professional training a central concern. Limited tuition happens, as the recipient, in all probability, will be insecure and resentful about the practice, thoughtlessly submitting to such demands.

Most situations leave the professional person to their own devices, none the wiser about their encounter with misadventure in accuracy, precision and clarity. Competent readers, if not professional peers, will have a number of genuine concerns, however. Professionals must be better positioned to demand more from their writing and less from their readers, for making their 'voice' heard much more strikingly.

In sport, John Whitmore in his book *Coaching for Performance* cites extensive research that shows that the state of mind of the performer is the key to the active performance of any kind, for which attitudes connected with awareness and responsibility particularly are crucial. It is through the fostering of awareness and the nurturing of responsibility that performance benefits. This applies as much to the professional person as any, who has to be no less competitive in many ways, such as in competing for the concentration of readers and for the acknowledgement of peers. A character of resourceful attention in attitudinal matters is absolutely essential for thoughtful conduct that yields accomplished writing.

When that character is suspect, the conscious knowing and understanding of awareness, as well as the responsive and answerable presence of responsibility, are underdeveloped. It is for that reason that most professional people, diffidently or unwittingly, are falling short in the performance challenge that is the writing task. How they fall short signals how not to be a thoughtless, slovenly writer.

Professionalism on the Page treats awareness and responsibility as the pillars of professionalism that support a platform for writing performance. Developing the right outlook or mindset in this respect is the way forward.

It is through virtual coaching and mentoring, not through heavily laden theory or training and style guides, not to mention endless rules of grammar, that a resourceful character is best developed. Imparting instructive experience through coaching unlocks the potential to maximise performance and, through mentoring, wisdom from a more experienced colleague (this author) is offered and an understanding shared. Capitalising on instructive experience in this way ensures that the writing task ceases to be set adrift from judicious thought. The professionally intent person will be orientated with an awareness and responsibility of mind, a mental acuity for resourceful, professional endeavour in the writing task.

The coaching and mentoring provided herein work by capturing relevant, extensive experience at the highest level in two ways. Firstly, all aspects of the writing task are given vivid, coherent expression akin to a hazardous vehicle journey, one in which the writer, as driver, must swiftly and safely transport an audience of readers to the goal destination of the writing task. Secondly, respective codes of conduct for awareness and responsibility are meticulously formulated in focussed layers, addressing particular concerns chapter by chapter. In subsequent chapters, these then inform writing performance by way of a method of approach and headline techniques.

The respective codes of conduct, the method of approach and the headline techniques will go a long way to furnish a character of resourceful attention in the professional person; they amount to the way of *Exact Writing*, which is the device of this author.

In the ensuing chapters, an experienced look at what is expected of professional people and how their written work falls short of the mark shows the damaging role of poor attitudes and what it takes to put matters right. Through instructive experience, crucial performance yardsticks become clear and an appropriate method of conduct for resourceful, professional endeavour presents itself for accomplished writing.

Summoning awareness and responsibility, not in a formulaic, mechanistic way, but in the practical structured framework that follows, is the key to successful performance. *Professionalism on the Page* makes sense of professional life. It shows especially the crucial importance of mind and method over misadventure, for accuracy, precision and clarity, not least in the interests of pursuing manageable brevity.

I. AWARENESS

JOURNEY ESSENTIALS

Awareness is the first attitudinal 'pillar of professionalism'. Having awareness, the professionally-minded person sees the measure of the writing task ahead with all that is involved in creating written work. Part I to *Professionalism on the Page* is about knowing what to expect – of the language medium, of yourself and of readers. It gives a working perspective view of the writing task.

The functions of prose (Chapter One), the attributes of professionalism (Chapter Two) and the parameters of readership (Chapter Three) each reveal the operational complexity of the writing task. Each chapter comprises a tranche or layer to a Code of Awareness.

Part I is the vehicle of the writing journey, its handling characteristics, motive force and capacity for carrying passengers that are to be transported.

Chapter One
THE VEHICLE OF PROSE

My task, which I am trying to achieve, is, by the power of the written word, to make you hear, to make you feel – it is, before all, to make you see.

Joseph Conrad 1857-1924
Polish-British author and a 'master prose stylist'

Concerns

Professionals are obliged to write for many important reasons, yet may fail to realise what power written work has. The writing task is serious, challenging and potentially immensely satisfying. Many will have long since forgotten when and how they learnt to read and write and, of course, will be in the habit of using those skills automatically without due interest, even after training in a chosen profession. Unfortunately, then, inadequate attention to written work is likely to ensue.

> What makes written work so important? What power is there and how is it used? How is written work to be viewed by the professional person so that others can see?

This chapter identifies the functioning of prose from the perspective of the writer, with particular reference to the written work of professional people. The use of the bold font gives emphasis to the first mentioning of each function.

Functions indicate the handling characteristics of the vehicle of prose for use in the writing journey.

Prose in a Different Light

Apparently, in William Shakespeare's day, there were 40,000 or so words in the English language and he mastered half of them. Today there are over 1,000,000 words. There is great scope for accuracy, precision and clarity in usage, but then, too, there is inordinate room for sloppiness. The language functions in choosing and arranging words across that considerable spectrum, with the power to influence our feelings and challenge our minds.

There are many thoroughly illuminating accounts of the origin, development and usage of English language, as well as of theory concerning the interpretation of English literature. These do not easily yield a simple operational view of the function of language, its workings from the perspective of the writer in the professional workplace, to know what the language does and does not do as a 'tool of the trade'. As a starting position, a foundation if you will, *Professionalism on the Page* brings that operational view into the light by drawing upon certain fundamentals of the language that are often obvious upon reflection, but unwisely and harmfully discounted, overlooked or otherwise neglected. Inevitably, some familiar groundwork is recognisable in the account that follows.

Speaking, Seeing and Hearing

In the DNA of the British are hundreds of lineages from all over the world. The history of immigration since the last ice age and the legacy of the British Empire have put the English language centre stage in enabling the communication of the most sophisticated of ideas, as well as the most complicated realities. English deserves great respect.

Words work in a particular way, which is thoroughly elucidated by Jay David Bolter in his book *Writing Space: The Computer, Hypertext, and the History of Writing*, amongst many others. These emphasise that language is about generating meaning. The writer mentally speaks thoughts when writing. The reader does not listen but seeks to hear through the eye, from what the page presents. Writing is about linking sounds to visual images. Many writers seldom attempt to see their work as the reader does, yet expect readers to hear the speaking of their voice as intended. This is the inescapable fact of the matter and the source of much difficulty.

Prose is a system by which readers verbalise sounds from sight to obtain meaning, namely to have an inner 'eye-voice' of the writer that is heard as the eye reads, usually one word at a time. If the reader is to hear words as intended, to see and feel meaning, there is a gap for the writer to bridge between the initial 'thought voice' and the 'eye-voice' it becomes. Advanced readers are able to go beyond hearing individual words by seeing clutches of words as images with meaning. Indeed, hearing is not the only way in which to read, and systems of symbols and pictures that show meaning without the use of sound were common in ancient times.

Reading by hearing is a different activity to listening through engaging in speech. Oral communication is spontaneous, dynamic and interactive. It heavily relies upon inflections (modulations of the voice), body language (especially gesticulation and facial expressions), feedback and response to get things right. With oral communication, each party understands what the other is saying, usually after several exchanges have yielded elaboration or clarification. Stripped of all those embellishments, understanding through speech becomes mostly inaccurate, imprecise and unclear.

In contrast, prose is premeditated, static and one-directional. Through writing, words are set down in a considered manner and deferred for later reading. There is a pervasiveness to prose as it communicates thoughts over time and place, subject to absent readers reactivating the words in the manner intended. With the aid of grammatical practices and conventions, the writer attempts to give readers guidance and instruction by how the content, form and structure of the text shapes meaning.

Guidance and instruction are not a straightforward matter, for there is a tension between two divergent approaches to what amounts to good English. In the traditional prescriptive approach, strictly followed learnt rules of grammar and punctuation, hundreds of them, stipulate the arrangement of words for correctness. This is often at odds with the contextual approach of more recent generations that follows appropriateness of usage from current experience as the mechanism for guidance and instruction of the reader; grammar has uncertain value, with limited attention given to solecisms (*errors in grammar*), provided the meaning is clear. Seemingly, there is an endless controversy about these approaches.

The traditional, prescriptive approach is termed *Standard English.* Linguists report that it came about during the eighteenth century when rich and powerful people wanted to distance themselves from all others who communicated with local dialects and accents. For the same reason, Standard English comes with a 'received pronunciation', with which any trace of local accent is subordinated or lost. The Standard English of that time was associated only with people in important positions in society, which largely continues to be so today. Standard English is a non-geographical dialect carrying most prestige, and it is unquestionably a 'rite of passage' for professional people.

English has evolved and mutated under many influences, notably historically those of the languages of invaders and raiders, and has continued to do so with immigration and travel in more recent times. Whatever approach is favoured, language usage inevitably changes over time. Usage changes slowly and resistively with the prescriptive approach, but more quickly and enthusiastically with the contextual approach.

The test of acceptability for change, in either case, is satisfied when common usage dictates, which is usually when an expansion of our power of written expression occurs. The writer must face up to the fact that English is not and never has been a managed language. There is no authority in control and the shifting tides of precedent and interpretation are all we have. Respected media (BBC and quality newspapers) and governmental documentation sometimes lead or resist those shifting tides.

Some observers are inclined to say that English is in a mess; others say it is in rude health, so long as users can go on abusing it, changing it in so many rich and varied ways. Members of each generation will make of the language what they will according to their circumstances and, as with music, it will come to serve them as they see fit; it is their language after all. They will force expressions into use and abandon others, despite protestations. The important point here, however, is that the professional person is not a free agent when it comes to language development and usage, for such persons have signed up to certain literary expectations and obligations: the 'rite of passage' above.

Caution is the watchword, especially in a world where acclaimed writers take the biggest chances with expression, in breaking conventions and the rules of grammar. It is worth realising that writers who do this successfully are usually experts in the conventions they are breaking. A writer who has achieved real mastery in the handling of words is sensibly justified in declining to be so fettered. Under no circumstances is this appropriate to the professional person, who in any event is unlikely to be such a master of the language.

In any case, freedoms are not without limitations or boundaries, and in that regard restraint on the unbridled development of English comes in various guises. There is, for example, the Queen's English Society, founded in 1972, that deplores declining standards in English and works to promote the maintenance, knowledge, development and appreciation of the language. It advises on correct usage and discourages anything detrimental, allowing the possibility for grammatical change. Additionally, there is the Plain English Campaign. Since its inception in 1979, the Plain English Campaign has gained a respected international reputation in providing services to businesses and advice to government departments and local authorities, offering the coveted 'Crystal Mark' for clear and unambiguous literature.

In this fluid and complex state of affairs, well-intended prose has an infinite **capacity** to attract confusion or criticism, or both, in some quarter or other. It is, nevertheless, a capacity for choice, arrangement and organisation of words with which to aid understanding and make the meaning clear. The writer must stay firmly in control of utilising that capacity. How the writer does that is down to individual style (much more about this in Part III).

Words and Connotations

The writer uses words as tools for conveying a thought to trigger a response in others. The communication of a thought in writing, once done, cannot go away; it cannot be 'un-thought'. Writing permanently influences the reader in some way or other, often in feeling or action; it has a powerful **force** that requires careful consideration. Notwithstanding the rules of grammar, even where ardently applied, there are problems with ambiguity, for there is no limit to what the writer is able to write.

When accuracy, precision or clarity of meaning is lacking, the force of prose is misdirected and the intended thought or message therein is corrupted and confused. A well-known example comes from the Charge of the Light Brigade of the British Army in 1854. Over 110 cavalry soldiers were killed and 160 wounded during the Crimean War in the Battle of Balaclava (of modern-day Ukraine, but recently annexed by Russia). The fatal consequences of a misdirected message of command led to an unintended frontal assault against entrenched artillery, rather than to the desired skirmishes elsewhere.

Additionally, words have connotations that convey good and bad messages. For example, a person is slim (good), or a person is skinny (bad). The poem *The Charge of the Light Brigade* by Alfred, Lord Tennyson vividly memorialises the battle and influences the reader through feelings rather than facts. By skilful use of carefully chosen words, the acceptable outcome of courage and heroism stands out, notwithstanding acknowledgement of the unacceptable military blunder.

Interestingly, too, the Crimean War is held to have given rise to the 'war correspondent'. Truth-telling accuracy from direct, first-hand reporting with precision and clarity gave an analysis of the events. The power of such reporting overcame potential Government subversion and propaganda at the time, as well as the tendency to write one-sided histories subsequently.

Language may be deliberately loaded with ambiguity when the writer seeks flexibility or 'wriggle room' in order to resist future commitment to a particular view or meaning when that would be unwise with the prospect of emerging evidence of more recent events. Politicians come to mind. In addition, prose may attempt to provoke strongly positive or negative reactions in order to persuade the recipient to some reaction or view. Wording that functions largely to sway or subvert emotions is loaded language. There is a routine use of this in advertising and it is the bedrock of conversation. It rests on the fact that an emotional response circumvents the need for argument or further considered judgement.

Extempore speakers aside, great speeches from skilfully written notes demonstrate the effect of emotional words. Emotional speeches have beneficially changed the course of history. An example, albeit one that departed somewhat from the prepared notes, is that by Martin Luther King. In 1963, his *I have a dream....* speech helped put American racial equality at the top of the agenda of reformers, and facilitated passage of the Civil Rights Act of 1964. It is a striking example of non-violent activism through the force of words.

However, emotion can be in serious contrast to an appeal to logic and reason. When that happens, impartiality and truth are likely to be casualties and it is inappropriate where objectivity is vital. Avoidance of emotive, loaded language can be extremely difficult because it can be subtle and neutral on first inspection.

Take this example: 'tax relief'. This, of course, refers to changes that reduce the amount a person must pay. Use of the word *relief* is emotive because it suggests that the person should feel all tax to be an unreasonable burden from which relief is welcome. The phrase is inaccurate about the tax system; it is imprecise about what is being relieved, and it is unclear about why it is a good thing. Through common usage, we cease to be aware of how it makes us think. Another example is when words such as 'deny', 'resist' and 'reject' are replaced with 'refute' (to repel), 'rebut' (to negate) and 'disprove' (to prove false) which encourage the reader to take sides in the matter.

Opposite to loaded language is legal prose, written for one interpretation only with faultless accuracy and compelling precision, irrespective of how difficult it may be to follow its meaning on a first reading. This is necessary so that no one is likely to succeed in persuading a court of law that the text bears a meaning other than that intended. It results in a cumbrous technical language of a distinct kind that adopts particular conventions of special meaning.

Certain other conventions of special meaning regularly amount to jargon. People first think of jargon as a private, precise technical language, but professional people, particularly, are prone to the use of non-technical jargon. Either way, it works well when the reader knows precisely what the writer meant by jargon expressions, but others not 'in the loop' of that communication are confronted with difficulty in understanding. Where all meaning is lost, 'gobbledegook' prevails.

Here is a recent example of 'political jargon' shown by John Humphrys in his excellent book *Lost for Words*, taken from *Modern Communications Operating Model* by the Government Communications Service (2015):

> The media industry's struggle to cope with a declining business model offers the opportunity for government to produce more direct-to-consumer creative content ... The opportunity is not so much about government pushing native content, rather about creating fully-fledged media production teams, sensitive to the nuances of each channel and audience.

There must be a better way of communicating the possible intended meaning, such as:

> As the advertising industry is no longer well suited to changing government needs, now is the time for new

internal media production teams to secure a better reach.

For particularly difficult examples, many readers will be inclined to accept the face value of what the writer has set down, in preference to an admission of 'not knowing'. Incentives to pretend are strong and it requires some degree of bravery to show one's ignorance. There is no question about this. For example, John Humphrys (above) reports that an American physicist, so disenchanted with the acceptance of overworked jargon, decided to demonstrate how vacuous yet pervasive it is by writing entirely in jargon and gobbledegook a meaningless article for an academic journal. The article became published and acclaimed!

Pretending to know inhibits evaluation or challenge of the content and source of written work. Some writers, academics, scientists and professionals alike gain benefit from this when jargon makes it hard for readers to understand meaning in their work. Others may deliberately seek this as a coping strategy, and then again, still others will unwittingly leave readers adrift. Sadly, many professionals freely engage in non-technical jargon, unwisely in the belief that it is integral to formal writing, which it is not.

All of this shows that there is boundless **versatility** to the force of prose, ranging from one extreme of being emotive and manipulative to the other of being utilitarian, technical or scientific, with jargon in both camps. In the face of all manner of temptations for less rigorous or obscure coverage, the versatility of prose can lead the writer seductively away from the objective impartiality of truth-telling accuracy with precision and clarity.

Through prose, the professional person must communicate with readers faithfully, not least because of its inherent significance.

Inherent Significance

Communication serves the intended purpose(s). The intended purpose of prose is to communicate thoughts and to speak with a voice through the persona of the writer. In professional life, there are many personas, disciplines from accountancy to veterinary practice. The mainstream communication of service professionals, as defined in the *Preface*, largely concerns subjects of **gravity** requiring careful deliberation, often with perspicacity. The communication of thoughts in that regard is for sharing an understanding, facilitating collaboration or prompting action.

Such communication centres upon addressing questions, issues and problems on behalf of a 'client' through variously engaging in these work areas:
- Concluding/Producing – material for information, assimilation or dissemination
- Reporting – an event or outcome
- Advising – on the effect or impact of some substantive matter
- Recommending – a decision or a standpoint
- Deciding – a scheme or a course of action
- Instructing/Consulting – fellow professionals and

others

- Contending/Presenting – argument to peers or others, including advocacy and representation in connection therewith, as with a Town Planner submitting written evidence at a local public inquiry, hearing or elsewhere.

Inevitably, most, if not all, of these work areas rely upon finished written material in some guise or other to impart the relevant content impressively in the best interests of the client. This may be termed generically as 'best advice'. *To convey best advice with influence* is what causes the writing task to be carried out; it is the writing purpose to deliver that key message in the written product. It is not a simple exercise to fulfil, as a lifetime of experience and countless examples testify.

Bill Bryson, in his book *A Short History of Nearly Everything*, cannot resist drawing attention to this extreme, historical example that hopelessly fails to convey serious conclusions. It is by James Hutton FRSE (1726-1797), the highly respected founder member of the emerging science of geology, about the origin of the Earth:

The world which we inhabit is composed of the materials, not of the earth which was the immediate predecessor of the present, but of the earth which, in ascending from the present, we consider as the third, and which had preceded the land that was above the surface of the sea, while our present land was yet beneath the water of the ocean.

Undaunted by the confusion and criticism it drew, Hutton went on to write several books in a similar vein, notwithstanding considerable editorial help!

Being influenced by best advice is but one of the several determinative considerations for the reader. Clients may have good reason not always to follow best advice, such as conflict (upsetting another matter), politics (insufficient support or assigned weight), timing (not now) and cost (unaffordable). The reader is open to influence in an honest and impartial way but not necessarily to persuasion for action or thinking in any particular way. Rather than persuasion, it is a question of convincing the reader that the best advice given is indeed sound; it must have believability (more about this in Part III).

The language of conveying best advice in a convincing way is opposite to the empty or exaggerated language to persuade. The language of persuasive advertising, for example, is usually devoid of information as words are given over to creating positive associations through imagery and do not give rise to argument or thought. Rhetoric is a skilled language that links thought to argument and is subtle as well as seductive in impressing the reader or listener. However, it often carries an implication of exaggeration. The language of the influence of the professional person links thought to the argument, without subversion.

In the prose of the professional person a message

of such gravity, concerning what the reader wants or needs, carries influence through a commanding **tone**. This reflects the writer's stature (or power) in terms of position or connections, control of information, resources, procedures or outcomes and superior knowledge. That stature impresses through customary literary skill.

Given the gravity of the work areas, significant outcomes are at stake for the client and most likely for several or many others. The trigger is usually the written product of the professional person. An outcome so triggered is likely to have a prevalent and even an enduring **impact**, directly or indirectly, upon people's lives.

To add to the seriousness of the matter, the writing task involves far more than a simple one-way process of communication. Experts say that thinking occurs through language and that writing has transformed human consciousness more than any other invention. Sir Ernest Gowers put it another way: "… it is only by clothing their thoughts with words that they can think at all". The observation that early childhood memory tends to occur with the development of language skills fits that view.

In that light, writing externalises thoughts and serves as both an extension and a reflection of the writer's mind. It enhances our capacity for reasoned argument and our ability to trace connections among disparate ideas. Without it, the literate mind would not and could not think as it does. Some say that a person with a scant vocabulary will almost certainly be a weak thinker, but the richer and more copious a vocabulary, the more fertile is likely to be the thinking.

That means that written professional work of any merit is very much the product of the handling of words (choice, arrangement and organisation) with precision and clarity to compel accurate thinking. How the writer does that is a matter of individual style within the bounds of professionalism. A written product gives **expression** to the intellect or mental character of the writer in that way. Thoughts, words and character are indivisible, as the ancient wisdom of rabbinic codes and law from the *Talmud* shows:

> Pay attention to your thoughts, because they become words.
> Pay attention to your words, because they become actions.
> Pay attention to your actions, because they become habits.
> Pay attention to your habits, because they become your character.
> Pay attention to your character, because it is your fate.

The page lays bare the writer in another way. Dialects and accents show there to be many articulations of English. With these, users have a common geographical identity, irrespective of the substance of what they are writing or saying. Common interests, such as sport, also prompt particular language. So, too, is the case with the use of Standard English. Variations in the use of Standard English occur according to the type of 'group' or profession the writer belongs to. Medical English is very different to architectural English, for example.

Given the gravity, tone, impact and expression of prose, a conscientious writer will attempt to give a good account of themselves in their written work. Many, however, fail to take stock of the intrinsic value of prose in that undertaking.

Intrinsic Value

Written work is not always central in the mind of the thoughtless professional person who often distances it from proper attention. Many see the writing task as an encumbrance of potential difficulty and personal jeopardy, something to avoid or gloss over, especially in the face of numerous other daily work demands. Greater attention is often given to team working, meetings and conferences, as these are either stimulating or safe places to be in when negative moods strike.

That situation is compounded by the harsh reality that key readers are compelled to read the written product and, as likely as not, will not receive it with any marked enthusiasm. Probable reader apathy and ingratitude certainly do not help the disdainful writer.

In meetings, the dynamic make-up of oral communication gives listeners the opportunity to affect the telling. Even so, being dynamic has its limitations. Precision and clarity with words suffer through immediacy, as there is little time to reflect or contemplate, and retractions and amplifications become necessary. With the exception of when there is a verbatim record, which is exceptional indeed at any meeting or exchange, oral communication evaporates and is lost to a wider audience not present in time or place.

With dynamic exchanges in meetings, there is fluidity towards focus and content. Without restraint, these provoke the straying into unexpected and in all likelihood unfamiliar waters, which means that accuracy becomes questionable. This fuels also time-wasting, which is well known. Furthermore, we do not remember very well something told to us at meetings (we remember as little as 10% after three months). Whatever amount is remembered, stories are remembered imperfectly, and so, too, will be the 'story' of proceedings at a meeting. Colleagues may well ask of each other upon the realisation that accounts differ, 'Did we go to the same meeting?'

In contrast to meetings, it is a fact that through well-written work readers are able to retain content with comparative ease. Prose facilitates reader **recollection**, making it an important communication medium in its own right. Additionally, the setting down of written text for later reading by others is under the exclusive control of the writer, which provides an opportunity for **contemplation** and reflection beforehand. Owing to the interdependency of words with thoughts, contemplation on the choice of words and their arrangement helps prompt accurate and precise thinking and leads to a robust written product.

Additionally, written products have a wide reach over time and many will enter the public domain at some point and become essential documents for the process of

validation of results, possibly involving accountability or technical audit of some nature. In that regard, a poor standard will diminish efficacy and the written product may well become challengeable in the eyes of the discerning or disgruntled reader. People at meetings do not hold so overtly to account the speakers they hear.

Challenges to the validity of a written product come in many guises. For example, through the Freedom of Information Act 2000, which creates a public right of access to recorded information held by public authorities, information may come to light that is at odds with the written product.

In the extreme, challenges may relate to negligence where codes of professional conduct have been breached. Particularly, this is where there is a breach of the duty of care to the client, a breach of confidence or misuse of any information, and, not least, an infringement of intellectual property rights. In law, negligence arises when mistakes occur and/or the task performed falls below the expected general standards of those within the same profession.

As a rule, the potential for claims of negligence will usually go hand in hand with the quality of written work, for that clearly expresses the intellect and identity of the professional person and reflects the command of the subject and work area in question. The writing task will always be at risk of straying into areas of potential challenge and the function or role of the written product to validate results and outcomes will become jeopardised.

As a safeguard, the professional person is required to

have continuous professional negligence insurance cover, to include a run-off period of six years upon retirement (in the case of the Royal Town Planning Institute).

The writing task may suffer in any number of ways when the writer does not entirely honour the functions of prose. This happens especially when there are time constraints and expediency takes over. The attraction of technologically driven language bears some responsibility for this.

Transmitted Words

In these times, professional work has a growing dependency upon electronic communication, notably with the use of SMS (text messaging) and e-mails. There is also computer hypertext, which is an electronic network of files that the user may structure at will. Transmitted words bring the benefit of fast and reactive delivery. Some researchers anticipate the demise of conventional writing.

In the interests of speedy exchanges, electronic mediums attract types of prose, mostly informal, with which there is an **ease** of effort and use. Confusing the issue somewhat is the creation nowadays of both conventional (printed) and transmitted (electronic) text at the computer screen (or tablet or smartphone).

Even with hypertext relating to a variety of prose, there is an ease of effort for the writer and reader both. Its non-linear structure provides a rich network of paths within and between works. The writer easily imports highly detailed and extensive material through amplifications and connections as hyperlinks, in place of what would otherwise be cumbersome footnotes and annexes to printed text. The reader variably sources the networked material just as desired, without complication and with ease.

Variably sourcing material through hypertext poses limitations, however. The reader's manipulation of the text to a final sought-after result will be unknown to the originating writer. The writer may skilfully direct the reader to some degree, but cannot be sure of the result and the reliance put upon it. There is an impermanence and changeability of the structures so created. Seldom is a single 'document' discernible and available for future use, such as in the function of validation.

The language of SMS has an extreme informality where the writer ventures to manipulate punctuation and spelling without loss of meaning, writing casually as in abbreviated speech. With SMS particularly, a virtual conversation takes place. There is a considerable **licence** for experimentation. Many observers bemoan the language of SMS on the grounds that, like it or not, one way that people are judged is how well they can spell.

Correct spelling is the mark of the educated person since the time when the English language ceased to be entirely and loosely phonetic, with different spellings according to accent. There are more sounds to it (40 in all) than the alphabet (26 letters). Spelling became standardised and respellings introduced owing to external influences of words from foreign languages entering English, which had unfamiliar and peculiar combinations of letters and sounds, and to etymological concerns. It has become a difficult but essential achievement because the incorrect spelling of the same-sounding words can alter meaning. The educational system continues to give great attention to it.

Other observers argue that texters need to be good spellers in order to know which letters to leave out. The brain's tendency not to read every letter by itself but the word image as a whole, often when first and last letters are in place, is what makes it work.

Here is a borrowed example from David Crystal's book *A Little Book of Language*:

> It *deosn't mttaer in what order the ltteers are, only that the frist and lsat ltter be at the rghit pclae, which is iprmoetnt.*

It is not always the case, however, that first and last letters be in place, as the following example shows:

> *I xpct yu cn read ths sntnce.*

Surprisingly, language manipulation involving disorganised spelling, or indeed no spelling at all, is not entirely a new skill.

David Crystal (above) reports that Queen Victoria, no less, delighted in puzzling over abbreviated language, which was termed a *rebus*. Here is a once popular example of a rebus:

Y Y U R Y Y U B I C U R Y Y 4 M E

This translates: too wise you are, too wise you be, I see you are too wise for me.

Correct spelling is often critical in professional life.

For example, a spelling mistake by the Government's Companies House, of just one letter in a business name, caused the eventual collapse of the company concerned with a loss of £9m and 250 jobs. Its existing and potential customers fled in the belief that it was on the verge of collapse, whereas the notice about impending liquidation issued by Companies House applied to a different business with a similar name.

That recently reported example reminds this author of when acting as a consultant on behalf the Government's Planning Inspectorate in a planning appeal case. Unhelpfully and unprofessionally, the written determination and decision then submitted for issue granted planning permission for a non-existent property, owing to a spelling mistake in the address details!

The casual, conversational type language of SMS can spill over into e-mails. Much of the language is at the mercy of trendy phrases, which first occur in conversation, then on radio and television and in films. Conversation laden with vogue terms is a kind of 'membership badge', which shows exclusivity and alienates the wider audience. In essence, these terms are new and poorly defined, being either euphemism, adopted jargon or errors in syntax (the structure of sentences). One thing is certain: words that do not expand the power of language but limit it do not last, notably when the writer uses words interchangeably and distinctions are lost. Unjustly or not, there is a risk that this casual, conversational form of prose will point to a lack of literary skill in the professional person.

The informal prose of electronic communication becomes problematic to the professional person in other ways. Firstly, it is very hard to establish a commanding tone to the written product. Secondly, when the typical one-to-one exchanges with known and trusted recipients escape the intended audience at some time, as they surely will, the conversational text will reach an audience for whom it is unsuited. Informality can be the tip of the iceberg of imprudence, as the numerous high-profile examples that reach the national press testify.

At the time of writing, the latest casualty is the Co-Chairman of Sony Pictures who has resigned in the wake of a leaked batch of office e-mails, insisting that she did not want 'to be defined' by their content. Readers will see, at least, a poor expression of the writer's intellect and identity, namely a poor professional image.

Lastly, ease of effort and use of informal prose potentially stimulate futility. A common experience amongst office workers is that e-mails induce futile transmissions through needless content and copying.

Each worker every year will receive many pointless e-mails, according to a recent poll as many as 1700. Copying messages to all parties on a precautionary basis, for them to be 'in the loop' so to speak, is behind some of it. It clogs inboxes as recipients struggle to find concise, ordered text and keywords to aid swift decisions on what to delete. Undisciplined, conversational writing that has few grammatical practices and conventions is the source of the difficulty. Uncertainty creeps in and recipients play safe by leaving messages active for potential future attention.

Many people believe the world of electronic communication to offer a less cumbersome language than that of conventional prose in printed documents. It is true that, in the wrong hands, the traditional, conventionally written prose of the professional person becomes unmanageably verbose and obtuse. However, when well written, it is concise and does not bar the use of an active voice for livelier sentences (more about this in Part III).

When using electronic communication, there is no necessity to give currency to what is novel. Indeed, as will become clear later, seldom will it be appropriate in professional circles to write so casually or generally in conversational, informal terms. Immediacy is not everything and the content is likely to benefit from contemplation and reflection. To 'write as you speak' is a popular trap because speech unfettered by the discipline of writing convention is often inaccurate, imprecise and unclear on first hearing.

Aside from poor accuracy, precision and clarity, and the missed opportunities for considered prose, when the professional person employs casual, conversational language, it will do justice neither to the gravity of the subject matter, nor to the impact upon people's lives. Furthermore, rigorous validation of the results for the task in hand will be jeopardised. As stated earlier, the professional person is not a free agent to play with language. Neither a leader nor a follower of the vogue must the professional person be, so not to suffer the consequences of inappropriate choice of words.

The professional who fails to write appropriately, to at least certain grammatical and other conventions that are a code of good manners for such written work, will cause offence. Do not be a rebel by giving currency to that which has not broken through the barrier of general consent. The discerning reader will be ever-present and will not tolerate such licence or indeed slip-ups of any kind. Technically incorrect language will interrupt and divert that reader's attention away from content, in most cases causing irritation and an impatience to dispense with the written product at the earliest opportunity.

A summary listing of the functions of prose appears in Table 1.

Table 1: Functions of Prose

capacity	)	HEARING and SEEING
force	)	
versatility	)	WORDS and CONNOTATIONS
gravity	)	
tone	)	
impact	)	
expression	)	SIGNIFICANCE
recollection	)	
contemplation	)	
validation	)	VALUE
ease	)	TRANSMITTED WORDS
licence	)	

Awareness – Seeing Word Power

Written products are arrangements of words of some capacity, force and versatility. Such constructions have particular significance and value to professional work, notably: significance through gravity, tone, impact and expression; and value through reader recollection, writer contemplation and result validation. Transmitted words are not necessarily set free of those functions, notwithstanding their attractive feature of ease of application for speed and the licence associated therewith. Transmitted informal text is ill-suited to set the professional person apart in kind and deed.

Insight

Written words in whatever medium require great care, respect and thoughtfulness in their handling. Thinking and writing are interdependent: one pushes the other AND vice versa. Thinking accurately and writing precisely with clarity, as professional people are required to do, is a very important challenge. The accomplished professional is in appropriate command of the language of the writing task by being effectively fluent (much more about this in Parts II and III).

Code of Awareness ~ Tranche 1: Linguistic Awareness

The manner in which the language of the writing task is to be regarded

Come to the writing task fully acquainted with the power of prose and a sense for commanding it appropriately, in the following manner:

- capacity – know the capacity of prose for confusion and criticism, ever-mindful of the value of practices and conventions that aid understanding, which bring it under control.
- force – be clear about the pragmatic motive to write and greatly respect the penetrating force of prose, on thought, action and feeling.
- versatility – be alert to the seductive versatility of prose for straying beyond the pragmatic through mistreatment, occasioning the risk of wayward results that frustrate or distort meaning.
- gravity – observe the gravity of the work in question and the need for impressive, commensurate best advice: accurate, precise and clear.
- tone – value the customary literary skill in Standard English for establishing a commanding tone to the written product.
- impact – understand the impact of the written product, directly or otherwise upon people's lives, realising their point of view.

- expression – be sure about the expression of personal intellect or mental character, in line with professional identity, that readers reasonably expect to be on show.
- recollection – appreciate what content readers are required to remember and how to assist them.
- contemplation – see contemplation as a prerequisite to a commitment to words, which inform thinking and vice versa in repeated cycles for their choice and arrangement.
- validation – beware the function of result validation, anticipating the risks of challenges, especially those due to the potentially damaging effects of time constraints.
- ease – distrust the ease of effort associated with much of the language of electronic communication, seeing the need to furnish equal attention on what to say and how to say it.
- licence – realise that the image arising from any electronic communication warrants restraint to at least that of an educated person with expertise, one in which such a person leaves aside the casual or conversational and novel usage of language.

Be mindful to handle the vehicle of prose with utmost care.

Chapter Two
THE ENGINE OF PROFESSIONALISM

Genius is nothing but labour and diligence.

William Hogarth 1697-1764
Political caricaturist

Concerns

Professionalism may not be genius exactly, but it does require a similar dedication. It is about high-quality performance attributable to professional ethics. High standards and more than average abilities in a particular field marks a person out as a 'professional'. In fact, too many fall short of the dedication to the mark of 'genius' when it comes to the writing task and fail to live fully up to expectations.

What can your client or the everyday person, or indeed your fellow professional truly expect of you, particularly through your written work, and you of yourself?

This chapter assesses the attributes of the professional person. As before, the use of the bold font gives emphasis to the first mentioning of these.

Attributes are the resources given to the vehicle of prose, its motive force.

Generic Assets

A professional is usually described to be a white-collar, graduate, qualified, and traditionally chartered person. That description is a starting point, for it belies the sophistication of the matter. It is through professional ethics that generic assets of personality, ability, judgement, conduct and literary skill of the professional person come to be engaged in an expected way. What the professional person brings to bear on the task in hand is a dedicated, comprehensive, directed effort through many attributes within those generic assets, honed by advanced education, training and experience. These define the make-up of the professional person. Those associated with personality greatly influence many attitudinal and behavioural responses to the task in hand.

Personality

A commonly held view is that certain attributes are largely the products of genetics. Some personalities are naturally predisposed towards professionalism. For example, a personality that positively reflects **conscientiousness** and an openness to experience is fully in tune with professionalism. Of all things, abundant motivation stands out. Psychologists, notably Eric Berne in 1964 and Abraham Maslow in 1970, have shown that motivation is substantially the product of human emotional needs, particularly those of gaining self-esteem and the esteem of others. The emotional need for esteem causes professional people constantly to prove themselves worthy or look to enhancing and acquiring skills. The inherent significance of the work involved, especially in terms of gravity and impact, helps in that regard (Chapter One ~ see *Inherent Significance*).

When the professional person engages in initial and continuing training, qualification and experience, self-esteem flourishes. With the attainment of widely acknowledged professional membership through those means, especially through a binding strict Code of Conduct, the competent professional person enjoys additionally the esteem of others. With self-esteem and the esteem of others so gained, the professional person has sound **emotional intelligence**.

Observers note that emotional intelligence is twice as important for success in the workplace as mental acuity. Clients and others expect at least as much from the motivation of a confident professional person with sound emotional intelligence as from the expert and specialised knowledge held. It amounts to authentic motivation through self-belief (an individual's internal drive), as opposed to artificial motivation through incentive schemes of one form or another.

A natural inclination for **resilience** helps motivation and is, more often than not, presumed in the professional person. Being cautiously optimistic to believe that things will work out well, in the end, is what it takes. The resilient professional has a steadfast determination to overcome setbacks of whatever nature, being prepared to learn from these with revitalised motivation for securing the best outcome.

Both emotional intelligence and resilience involve self-analysis and mounting personal standards, behaviour that tends to be reinforced through ability (below). Aside from the emotional need for esteem, there will be 'growth needs' from a desire for personal development. In all this, the competent professional person is inclined to be habitually not satisfied by – albeit not necessarily *dissatisfied* with – their performance, unless convinced that the best possible outcome in the circumstances has been achieved. Just enough to get by is never good enough.

Some observers liken such motivation to perfectionism. Perfectionists are highly motivated by a need to consistently prove themselves. Even though professional people may seem to be so inclined, recent research published in *Personality and Social Psychology Review* indicates otherwise. It finds that perfectionists are unable to cope well with demands and uncertainties in the workplace, and points out that such observers regularly confuse perfectionism with conscientiousness.

Nevertheless, conscientiousness will tend to make professional people their own harshest critic. That is not to say that a form of self-doubt and a lack of self-belief become manifest, but rather that a challenging, purpose-driven approach sets a high standard. There is likely to be plenty of scope for meeting such challenges. Typically, a person has dormant capacity as, according to some researchers, one releases only 40% of one's potential in the workplace.

Conscientiousness, emotional intelligence and resilience give vigour to the work of the professional person and facilitate ability.

Ability

A professional person is required to have expert and specialised **temporal knowledge**. This is knowledge about the subject (your discipline), the field (your specialism) and the job in question (your expertise about how to tackle it), all of which are impressively communicated in written work.

Greatly associated with professional competence is **critical thinking**, which is an important intellectual ability of most professional disciplines. Critical thinking results from asking questions, examining a matter from all possible angles and positions. The focus is in the habitual practice of being open-minded, analytical, inquisitive and experimental. Crucially, it is about being willing and able to evaluate one's thinking: to engage in reflective thought. Through critical thinking, the professional person has an awareness of the fitness of expert and specialised knowledge.

It is through **reasoning** that the professional person strives to move compellingly towards a conclusion, by establishing positive evidence and negating oppositional evidence (a balanced weighing up). Reasoning is the lifeblood of the professional person. According to the *Oxford English Dictionary*, to reason is to *form or try to reach conclusions by connected thought.* Reasoning carries critical thinking along the route of its inquisitorial journey, connecting one thought with another, involving analysis-synthesis-evaluation.

Reasoning through critical thinking happens resourcefully or experimentally with such characteristic practices as skipping steps, working backwards, looking at examples or seeing what happens if you change things. Evidence of one form or another always underpins reasoning.

The fundamental point is that there is no place for mere assertion, which has inadequate recourse to thought, observation or reason. Behind a professional opinion is a sound analysis of source material, the synthesis and evaluation of multiple sources of which are usually required. This provides 'evidence' for enabling reasoning to determine or demonstrate the truth of an assertion. It comes in various forms, from the scientific basis of empirical data to the personal basis of experience through judgement.

Judgement

Judgement is the product of reasoning. In town planning and sister professions, reasoning expressed in much written work lies beyond *deductive* or logical thought (the scope for which is limited by the subjective character of evidence) and is often *inductive* in nature, relying on probabilities. Deductive reasoning reaches logically certain conclusions, whereas with inductive reasoning the truth of a conclusion rests on the strength of evidence, which does not provide absolute proof. Unlike deductive reasoning, inductive reasoning is either weak or strong, which accounts for how probable it is that the conclusion is true.

There is a whole raft of evidence types: circumstantial, documentary, presumptive and collateral, to name but a few. The crux of the matter for the professional person is that it is unwise to attempt to reason without significant inputs of facts or accredited information. The appropriate assembling of these inputs benefits from experience. Through experience, the professional person has a latent force of **practical intelligence** that enhances the calibre of reasoning engaged in to reach the requisite standard of evidence.

Additionally, having a base of well-established experience assists the professional person to bring considerable insight to bear on the work in question. Insight is a hidden truth, about knowing without external proof. **Instinctual knowledge** gleaned from intuitive insight is untraceable, coming as it does from the creative, imaginative area of the brain. It is where the subconscious mind brings things into existence by the sheer power of thought. However, through engaging in 'back-reasoning', the professional person can uphold the linear and logical processes of reasoning. Working backwards in this way is very much part of critical thinking.

Instinctual knowledge is powerful. Apparently,

from those involved with intuitive training, it accounts for 90% of the power of the brain, and some even say that it has infinite resources at its command, including accumulated wisdom. The common notion that the 'left cortex' of the brain is the academic side, handling logic and numbers particularly, and the 'right cortex' is the creative side, handling imagination, including intuition and the like, is misleading. Academic and creative success results from combining linguistic, numerical and analytical skills with imagination: both sides of the brain. Albert Einstein, no less, has stressed the importance of imagination in the academic world, stating that it is more important than knowledge, for many great discoveries have occurred through such 'creative leaps' in reasoning from intuitive insight.

In the world of instinctual knowledge, when intuitive insight occurs, it is called the 'twilight state'. This is where the mind passes through when a person gently and freely drifts off to sleep or wakes from a dream; it is where theta brainwaves predominate to yield vivid memories, sudden insights and creative inspiration. Some people practise theta meditation to intentionally induce those results and, with further reference to him, Albert Einstein could often do so when seeking creative insights in his work. If reasoning is the lifeblood of the professional person, then instinctual knowledge is the soul. The value of the twilight state to the professional person must never be underestimated.

Being able to derive an expert opinion augmented by experience – practical intelligence and instinctual knowledge – is to apply independent professional judgement, which makes the professional person highly respected. An expert opinion based upon such judgement is an opinion that the professional person is entitled to hold. A court may take this as evidence as if it were fact, for it has credibility through its source. In court or inquiry proceedings, this would be subject to testing (of expertise) and/or cross-examination (exploring contrary opinion). In all civil proceedings, the standard (of proof) required would be on the balance of probabilities.

The professional person is there to assist the proceedings to receive all relevant 'factual' material and to draw conclusions from it. It is for the advocate dealing with testing/cross-examination to get at the core of the evidence by exploring especially the matter of credibility of the source, as well as matters of validity and probability. A 'witness' who thinks about a question is always an impressive witness, whereas a witness who is quick to respond and careless in the choice of words will be discredited. To be able to deliver expert opinion soundly requires accurate thinking, the basis for which is in the written statement, due to the inherent significance of prose in enabling thought (see Chapter One: *The Vehicle of Prose*).

For those reasons, the calibre of the reasoning behind professional judgement is not only about content, as from practical intelligence and instinctual knowledge, but also about **composure** concerning how it comes across to all parties involved. For it to have any real worth, the independent professional judgement of the professional person comes with a cool, calm, confident bearing, showing a considered, collected approach. Self-assurance is what it takes to be composed.

With inductive reasoning, then, the reader must be satisfied that the matter has been established to be more likely than not. Stating something to be 'likely' or 'possible' invites actual or virtual challenges to see if something else is 'more likely', for which due acknowledgement is deserved. Questions such as these go to the very heart of reasoning and the standard of proof. The professional person must be fully cognisant of such potential questions and anticipate them through critical thinking.

The experience-based evidence is very important. Experience contributes to wisdom concerning how to employ knowledge. Wisdom tells us that it is wise to know what is best worth knowing and to do what is best worth doing. In addition, it tells us that failure is the key to success as it is the product of gainful experience.

The membership requirements of the Royal Town Planning Institute (RTPI) firmly reflect the importance of relevant experience. Obtaining membership involves an Assessment of Professional Competence, which embraces a Practical Experience Statement and a Professional Competence Statement (case studies). After recognised academic achievement, the candidate for membership must keep a logbook for submission to show at least two years of experience in a professional environment.

The Assessment criteria range from an understanding of context to an awareness of frameworks and challenges.

They include an ability to identify and analyse issues, competence in gathering appropriate information, and competence in identifying and evaluating a course of action.

The critical and balanced weighing up of the available, often incomplete or contradictory evidence to form a decision or opinion is what leads to independent professional judgement, cautiously and scrupulously derived. The RTPI Code of Professional Conduct requires that Members "shall fearlessly and impartially exercise their independent professional judgement to the best of their skill and understanding".

Practical intelligence and instinctual knowledge, generated through experience, define the expertise of the professional person as much as anything else. However, professionalism is also very much about obligations concerning conduct.

Conduct

Great faith is in the hands of the professional person and, commensurately, professional membership carries strict codes of conduct. The RTPI Code states that Members "shall act with **competence**, **honesty** and **integrity**", and are required to take all reasonable steps to maintain their professional competence throughout their working lives. The codes of various other professions reflect much about the same obligations.

Professional competence involves choice and a focus on how much or how little to do, as well as how to do it. It is attained particularly through the attributes of emotional intelligence, conscientiousness, knowledge, critical thinking, reasoning and practical intelligence. Ownership of the resultant output material is an integral obligation of professionalism. Even when working corporately or bureaucratically, the professional person is so obligated, insofar as their involvement indicates.

Being answerable through ownership of the content of the written product reflects the gravity of the work in question affecting people's lives. Particularly, it reflects a general duty of care to the client. This is an ethical duty to protect the client's best interests. Professional ethics bring to the fore honesty (not to deceive) and integrity (firm in principles). In exercise of that ethical duty, the professional person brings to bear **diligence**, supported by emotional intelligence and resilience of personality. These give a high work ethic in the form of perseverance and industry, which is especially useful in the realm of critical thinking.

Being duty-bound in this way is not only about doing things right, it is about doing the right thing and is central to professionalism. A professional person is a dedicated person having freely accepted responsibility (more about this in Part II). It is wholeheartedness, which is quite different to a given or imposed responsibility that merely makes possible independence of action with executive power.

The general duty of care to the client is an irresistible force on the conduct of the professional person, particularly because it operates in a 'push and pull' capacity ('carrot' and 'stick'). The pull force (the 'carrot') exists in the form of a satisfied client, in addition to personal fulfilment through esteem and growth needs. The push force (the 'stick') is something akin to 'fear of failure'. At the extreme, it concerns negligence.

A fear of failure focuses the mind on doing well and successful people report that they experience this emotion more strongly than that of the desire or satisfaction of succeeding. However, some businesses see the fear of failure in their employees as an unhelpful burden when it engenders a lack of confidence and a self-doubt that inhibit vital innovation. Others actively encourage it to promote innovation on the basis that success often comes after repeated failures. Either way, the professional person is largely fear-driven (more about this in Part II).

Professionalism is very much about the desire not to fail the client-employer and tarnish one's own stature: to be purpose-driven to do a job well alongside a positive outlook towards the work concerned and the profession in question. Overall, professional conduct ensures a confident keenness about what is to be done and how, with a wholehearted determination for faultlessness and excellence. In written work, this must manifest itself transparently through truth-telling accuracy, reported with precision and clarity.

Literary Skill

With reference to the functions of prose identified earlier, the message of best advice of the professional person is derived from unbiased analysis through an honest and dispassionate approach. Foremost in the customary literary skill of professional people is in the demonstration of **objectivity**.

The magnitude of the writing task in that regard cannot be overstated. Logical, accurate thinking and a precise choice of words with a clear way of handling them, communicate what and how the writer draws from a foundation of knowledge and experience. Writing makes it easier to see logical relationships and engage in critical thinking and reasoning, specifically through deductive, inductive and intuitive means. It provides an opportunity for analysis and reflection – the literate mind being analytic and objective.

Writing in that way is unquestionably a 'tool of the trade', very much the instrument of professionalism.

When applying the instrument of professionalism, writers reveal a lot about themselves. Through written work, professionalism expresses itself with a voice before an audience. That voice must carry some influence so that the written product has the power to affect readers, their ideas, images, thoughts, feelings and actions. Releasing that power is likened by theorists to 'weapons of influence', three of which apply here (Robert Cialdini, American social psychologist ~ *Theory of Influence*).

Firstly, readers are inclined to obey **authority** figures. For the professional person, certain positional authority comes about in line with those work areas of an 'official' or bureaucratic nature, such as advising, recommending and deciding. Mostly, however, the fully competent professional person is an acknowledged subject matter expert through membership of a professional body. Professionalism so acknowledged carries its own traditional 'authority', to which customary literary skill is expected to do justice.

Readers will follow people they like. The person who presents a message can have a dramatic impact on its reception. Secondly then is **courtesy**, which fosters likeability. Showing courtesy by being objective, polite and considerate of all points of view is much more than a sentimental nicety. Courtesy cultivates goodwill and lessens the potential alienation or hostility of the reader. At the very least, it is courteous through literary skill to not leave readers in search of the meaning that is intended. Ideally, the professional person becomes 'liked' by earning respect for the handling of a job well done. It is difficult not to like a person whom you have come to respect.

Lastly, readers do not like to be self-contradictory without good reason. In other words, they will have a commitment to their view and to all that is associated with it. The professional person must communicate to readers good reason to change course against their natural inclination. Through customary literary skill, readers will be prepared to see the writer as genuine and sincere, a reliable source of expertise who can be trusted. The **legitimacy** or rightfulness of the professional person as a credible source is signified and, if executed well, offers a good reason to readers for a self-contradictory change.

There is no room for a feeble approach that jeopardises the customary literary skill of the professional person. Customary literary skill is that through which the objectivity, authority, courtesy and legitimacy of the writer are communicated, and it is a benchmark of professionalism: it is the starting position for the accomplished professional (more about this in Part II).

A summary listing of the attributes of professionalism appears in Table 2.

Table 2: Attributes of Professionalism

conscientiousness	)	
emotional intelligence	)	
resilience	)	PERSONALITY
temporal knowledge	)	
critical thinking	)	
reasoning	)	ABILITY
practical intelligence	)	
instinctual knowledge	)	
composure	)	JUDGEMENT
competence	)	
honesty	)	
integrity	)	
diligence	)	CONDUCT
objectivity	)	
authority	)	
courtesy	)	
legitimacy	)	LITERARY SKILL

Awareness – Understanding Stature

Professional attributes are manifold and empower the personality, ability, judgement, conduct and literary skill of the professional person. They range from emotional intelligence to legitimacy, and fusing them all is the professional hallmark of accurate, precise and clear, thoughtful expression. Poor or misguided literary accomplishment is harmful to professionalism as much as it is to the purpose of the written product.

Insight

The professional person is one with unimpeachable stature. It is no wonder that many professionals fall short of the mark when there is parsimonious effort given to the writing task in hand. Unlike most written communication completed without further ado, professionally it has a widespread run-on effect, namely: 'documentation' (the written product) – interrogation – reputation. The accomplished professional draws upon a whole array of substantial attributes to resource the writing task in a predictably reliable way, not least with a positive outlook and a purposeful intent (much more about this in Parts II and III).

Code of Awareness ~ Tranche 2: Self-Awareness

The resources with which the writing task is to be engaged

Engage in the writing task in hand, no matter how slight, as an exercise in professionalism, and greatly value it with these resources brought to bear as follows:

- conscientiousness – be purpose-driven with conscientiousness for mounting personal standards with relentless self-criticism, line by line and word by word.
- emotional intelligence – let emotional intelligence impart a confident, positive outlook for doing well and look always to strengthen self-belief.
- resilience – believe in the best possible outcome from any given situation with a determination to learn from and overcome any setbacks.
- temporal knowledge – ensure that the requisite temporal knowledge about the subject, field and work in question is on hand.
- critical thinking – be poised for critical thinking to be second nature to temporal knowledge, for accurate, authentic content.
- reasoning – be ready with reasoning to firmly connect thoughts with a balanced weighing up of content.
- practical intelligence – draw from a fund of practical intelligence to enlighten analysis, synthesis and evaluation.
- instinctual knowledge – capture the twilight state of

mind to profit from instinctual knowledge through intuitive insights and creative leaps in reasoning, accommodated through back-reasoning.

- composure – apply composure with a self-assured, considered and collected approach.
- competence – engage competence with a clear understanding of the focus to bring to bear on the 'what' and 'how' of the demands of the subject.
- honesty – stick to professional ethics (rights and wrongs) at every juncture, for honest endeavour in all respects.
- integrity – harness a consistency of actions through firmly applied principles of unquestionable integrity.
- diligence – follow the client's best interests (in whatever form and direction the brief takes) with diligence so that the task is executed as well as it can be, with nothing overlooked.
- objectivity – present objectivity fully, in line with dispassionate, impartial conduct.
- authority – communicate positional or other authority for maximum influence.
- courtesy – show courtesy to readers, especially in the interests of negating potential hostility towards the written product.
- legitimacy – use customary literary skill to reinforce the legitimacy behind what is expected of readers.

Be the person it takes to empower the vehicle of prose.

Chapter Three
THE WEIGHT OF READERSHIP

By failing to prepare you are preparing to fail

Benjamin Franklin 1706-1790
American politician

Concerns

As is well known, the starting position for preparation of written work is to be mindful of your reader. That is undoubtedly true, but it is misleading and unhelpful if not fully understood. Those who are prone to pay scant attention to the readership (the audience body of all the various readers of your work), fail to understand its complexity and burden, with woeful outcomes.

> What will readers require of your written work and what does that mean for carrying out the writing task in hand? What manner of scrutiny by readers is likely that actively burdens the writing task?

This chapter examines the body of readers with reference

to parameters (or controlling variables) that define its characteristics and domain. As with the previous chapters, the use of the bold font gives emphasis to the first mentioning of these.

Parameters define the passengers the vehicle of prose is to carry, its payload.

Communication Requirements

A definition of reading is 'understanding what the author intended'; another is 'the assimilation of printed information'. Either way, reading is all about interpretation in the face of so many words competing for attention on the page.

In the exalted world of literature, there are a great many ways of interpreting the text, which are mostly valid and helpful. These reflect two divergent and contentious approaches about the position of the author. One places the author centrally as an artist of genius, to appreciate aesthetic work of its own right; the other puts the author in context, rather as an unwitting representative or agent of personal and political or cultural matters, to evaluate influences and insights in the work. The former is a traditional, inward-looking or *intrinsic* view; the latter is an outward-looking or *extrinsic* view.

This means that the same text may impress one reader yet disappoint another. Particularly with such divergent approaches, there are multiple and often unclear meanings of phrases, even of each word. The crux of it rests upon the degree to which the reader seeks out author-intention, especially when ambiguities abound, which may be intentional or not on the part of the author.

In the more commonplace pragmatic world of official and other utility writing, the subject matter of *Professionalism on the Page*, the writer must endeavour to orientate readers to make the intended interpretation only in order for the writing purpose to be fulfilled (Chapter One ~ see *Inherent Significance*). Readers will be looking for writer-intention: what the writer meant.

Meaning passes between the person of the writer and that of the reader. There is a geographical and temporal communication gulf that the writer must bridge. In the act of writing, the writer externalises thoughts as phrases, deferring them for later reading by others. The reader, however, has no choice other than to reactivate the words in the phrases; writers set down phrases but readers will read words (see ahead to *Reading Habits*). It is the writer's challenge to guide or equip readers so that they reactivate the words as intended.

Readers will thereby expect to feel the writer's **presence** strongly in the form of the artistry of everyday literary skill. Additionally, through that artistry, they will expect to be satisfied with the professional stature on offer (Chapter Two ~ see *Literary Skill*). They will not expect to see, or indeed find, contextual influences, but will be alert to the possibility of these as a sign of professional misconduct concerning objective impartiality. The presence of the writer must be worthy of the writer's professionalism, unencumbered and untainted by extraneous matters as far as possible.

In the act of interpretation, the reader reads written work with those expectations of the text, but also with presuppositions about it and the subject. Presuppositions are the ideas, tendencies and preferences that the reader brings to the table, and act as 'mental filters', selecting what information to take in. Expectations and presuppositions thereby shape interpretation.

Interpretation can be an intensely personal affair for readers, shaped by their expectations and presuppositions, established from their experiences, values, beliefs and prejudices. Even so, readers will receive the product of utility writing in a certain number of identifiable ways. Those ways concern the demands, interests, habits and capacity of readers (the paragraph headings below). Readers will scrutinise the written product accordingly and reactivate the words (fully or not) as they see fit, subject to what guidance the writer gives.

The professional person as a writer must think carefully about who is reading and how they read in order to frame the written product for the best chance of fulfilling its purpose. It is not just the writer's presence the reader must feel, but also very much the readers' presence the writer must feel. Writing sensitively in a non-blinkered manner is essential to the interpretation of intended meaning.

Mahatma Gandhi put it this way: "There is not a moment when I do not feel the presence of a witness whose eye misses nothing and with whom I strive to keep in tune." Experts in other circles liken it to writing with 'a judge looking over your shoulder', ready to intercede as and when necessary.

The accomplished writer is never alone in the writing task, standing simultaneously on both sides of the communication gulf to become a reader, too, long before engaging the readership. The **handling** of meaning is a joint affair, a sharing between the writer and readers. The pre-existing meanings and connotations of words shape what the writer has to say, sometimes with dire consequences (Chapter One ~ see *Words and Connotations* and *Transmitted Words*).The writer must exercise literary skill so not to lose essential control of meaning. In other words, the professional person must write to offer readers the best opportunity for them to become fully attuned to the written product.

Clients' Demands

Amongst the many eyes who miss nothing, the strongest presence is that of the client, with whom the writer must stay in tune. Paradoxically and inexcusably for some, it may be unclear who the client is. Undoubtedly, the professional person will be working for a client, whether for an individual or a corporate or public body, directly or indirectly. There will be certain instructions, formless or otherwise, relating to doing the job(s) in question. At best, a brief will present issues and material facts in some form or other and make known the client's position in the work in question. As well as seeking the substantive or technical content, the brief will go a long way to revealing the literacy demands upon the written work so engaged.

However, facing the professional person at the outset

with stubborn regularity is a very rudimentary picture, which may be inconsistent, incomplete, inaccurate and often dynamic (a 'moving target' through changing circumstances). Feedback is critical to communication between parties, and in the situation here it establishes the provenance of the 'brief' in whatever form it is to take. The professional person must examine and explore the brief with the client, not only initially, but also continually throughout the writing task in order to become fully cognisant of all demands. With objects and issues of the brief firmly and currently in view, a framework of **causation** surfaces for attention. This gives emphasis to the context and allows focus onto the scope of the work in question, within which detailed tasks may be adapted and refined to suit.

The professional person is acting in the best interests of the client by giving advice of an independent and impartial nature (Chapter Two ~ see *Judgement*). The client is a pre-eminent reader of unique importance, but there are likely to be a good many other important readers upon whom the fulfilment of the brief may well depend. This means the professional person is not necessarily writing *for* the client so much as writing on *behalf* of the client, in order to influence all relevant interested parties.

Readers' Interests

Interested parties are manifold. As readers, they will be inclined to analyse, criticise, appreciate, select or reject what they see according to their affairs; they will receive, evaluate and synthesise the written product. Basically, they will read for a *reason*, with a *mode* of reading adopted to suit both the subject and the reader. A level of *capability* of understanding is on hand and some form of *stimulus* to apply reading effort galvanises the whole. Additionally, the reader approaches the work with preconceptions that determine the *disposition* towards the written product.

Particularly, given the type of work of the professional person, the written product will be prone to some sort of interrogation or challenge from readers, from minor clarification or disagreement to procedural, technical or legal disputes of a formal kind.

Those reading traits affirm the readers' interests. The readership body is likely to bring various levels of interest to the reading table. These respective levels of interest establish the **temperament** that certain readers will have towards the written product. By gauging the different temperament of readers, the writer is able to experience the presence of the readership body more directly than otherwise. There are several potential levels of interest within each reading trait, as follows:

Reason (What do I want to get from this?)
- Enlighten   = *to learn something from an inquisitive standpoint*
- Inform   = *to be apprised of something for consideration*
- Actuate   = *to be directed towards some action, decision or opinion*

Mode (What attention am I going to give it?)
- Casual = *without great care, attention to detail or thought*
- Careful = *with a strong connection or interest*
- Forensic = *with detailed (scientific) scrutiny*

Capability (What do I already know?)
- Everyday = *that of a layperson*
- Knowledgeable = *that of an informed person*
- Professional = *that of a qualified person, having recognised expertise*

Stimulus (Why am I reading this?)
- Choice = *undertaken voluntarily for personal reasons such as self-development or pursuit of a cause*
- Opportunity = *unintentional sight of the written product that triggers curiosity and investigative tendencies*
- Reaction = *undertaken in response to some stimulus such as a development proposal*
- Compulsion = *undertaken through obligation in some capacity (e.g. employment, assignment, commission)*

Disposition (How do I feel towards it?)
- Friendly = *supportive*
- Ambivalent = *open-minded*
- Hostile = *critical/challenging*

Temperaments express what the reader is seeking from the written product and how; they express the communication gulf profitably for attention by the writer. To know your reader(s) is a complex matter, because in professional work there is seldom a single temperament or a uniform body of readers, unlike with most academic or scientific work.

Connecting with readers is crucial for fulfilling the writing purpose, about conveying a message of best advice influentially. The anticipation of temperament, including that of the client, is to exercise great care with the functions of prose when constructing and organising text. Writers must be in tune with their readership. Though daunting, it is an inescapable integral step in the writing task.

Below is an example of where several reader temperaments can surface, typical of the readership of the professional town planner working in a development control sphere of local government.

Example: Readership Temperaments of a Town Planner

1) *The developer-applicant as reader*
This reader has the *compulsion* to read from a *knowledgeable* or *professional* standpoint, being poised to seek to *actuate* matters in the desired direction, giving written material in connection therewith *careful*, if not *forensic* attention with a potentially *hostile* disposition.

2) An inexperienced resident as reader
This reader is curious and *ambivalent*, looking for the written material to *enlighten* or *inform*, reading by *opportunity* or *choice* in a *casual* manner with *everyday* capability.

3) An affected neighbour as reader
Through *reaction*, this *hostile* reader brings *careful* inspection of an acquired *knowledgeable* kind to *actuate* a preferred outcome from potentially adverse written material.

4) The planning committee (client) as reader(s)
These readers have the *compulsion* to read material in a *careful* and *knowledgeable* way with a *friendly* disposition in order to *actuate* an acceptable result or outcome.

Those temperaments may be joined by others subject to the calibre and resources of the applicant, appellant or resident, and the focus of various sister professions if they became drawn in. Aside from the client, many temperaments are important as nos. 1) and 3) in the above example indicate; each has the potency to shape matters differently when the written product fails to convince and carry influence. The harsh reality, however, is that the writer is not aware of some or several of the reading temperaments that will come into play. Seldom is the gulf between writer and reader fully bridged as a result.

For some work, the professional person will not be expected to be cognisant of all the relevant temperaments in play, or potentially so. For example, when the professional person acts as a decision-maker the courts have held that '…the reasons (for the decision) need refer only to the main issue in the dispute, not to every material consideration'. At the opposite end to this, for work areas such as *recommending* or *producing*, to not know the temperament of readers is to be unable to anticipate what is expected of the written message and the best means by which it may carry influence.

In this somewhat cloudy area of trying to determine temperaments, striking a suitable **alignment** is difficult. The challenge is to write the intended meaning in a discerning way, to reach the eclectic readership productively. The key is to strive to embrace firmly all main, existing and potential temperaments, leaving any clearly indicated peripheral ones to a lighter touch. The practical intelligence of the professional person greatly assists this process (Chapter Two ~ see *Judgement*).

The need for a suitable alignment is not to be underrated. When readers are disappointed with the message conveyed they are much less likely than otherwise to be content about the written product. Irrespective of whether these readers have main or peripheral temperaments, they require special attention in order to avoid disillusionment and potential follow-on proceedings or correspondence. The writer must 'write for the losing party', to address their principal concerns and leave them resigned to the fact that there is a good reason for the message to be as it is and not as desired, expected or indeed anticipated. This is not to say that the writer goes looking for issues.

Alongside all of this are 'hidden agendas' of a personal nature when readers just do not wish to be receptive (much more about this in Parts III and IV).

Reading Habits

Common to all reading is the habitual **inclination** of readers, through training, experience or practice, to apply a favoured method of reading to written work. Often this will reflect ability and personal circumstances. Respecting the method of reading of the candidate readers is something the professional person often overlooks when carrying out the writing task. Nevertheless, this parameter has great bearing on how well readers receive the written product.

Individual reading methods may be classed as follows, keeping in mind that readers are likely to use or attempt to use, one with another:

- **Mental Speaking or Sub-vocalisation**
  The reader silently speaks every word of the text at an even pace in their mind (the speed of speech).

- **Speed Reading**
  The reader uses the speed of the eye over the text (not that of speech) looking for word images, which involves degrees of scanning and skimming. In both, the eye runs rapidly over the text spotting punctuation cues, topic sentences, signpost words and word clusters.

- **Skip Reading**

  The reader is selective, searching for and being content to absorb parts of the text only, which may involve some skimming and scanning.

- **Critical or Close Reading**

  The reader advances through the text by focusing attention on particular parts of it whilst holding other information in mind, from which analysis, reflection, evaluation and judgements flow.

Proficient readers with experience may well sometimes be able to put aside their favoured habitual behaviour and respond to written work with a method most suited to the difficulty of the subject matter and content. This approach applies a **strategy** for reading.

Where the writer is able to give attention to and respect inclinations and strategies towards reading, the written product will assist the reader to navigate swiftly and successfully through the text, to read and process it without difficulty.

Reading Capacity

Prose that respects readers' interests and habits will be appealing, but it will not necessarily convey the message as intended. Reading capacity, especially in professional circles, is about quick understanding, which is dependent upon **concentration**, a basic parameter of readership. Concentrating or paying attention long enough is difficult for the reader. That is because attention is dynamic (it wanders), is undivided (inability to take in more than one thing at a time) and follows interest (boredom extinguishes attention). The writer must overcome reader impatience, fatigue or boredom.

Blockages to reading capacity occur when attention is lost or undermined. They come in many guises, not least through the environmental and other factors of the workplace. Distractions and interruptions create dispersed attention and a difficulty in maintaining focus. Alongside dispersed attention, readers' concentration may become strained by contextual difficulties concerning the subject matter; the reader may well ask 'what is the relevance of this to me?' Any reader difficulty with unfamiliar constructions or vocabulary, especially with corporate preferences or tendencies (jargon), compounds these problems.

Readers will respond to blockages in numerous ways. Note-taking, diagrams and mind maps are devices that greatly assist the reader in making progress through a difficult written product. Traditional note-taking mimics the familiar hierarchical, linear and logical structure of official or utility writing: from the general to the specific. Mind mapping, in contrast, mimics the working of the brain whereby the reader searches for and gathers an image from the substance of the written product, in part or completely, and places it centrally on the notepad, from which associative messages and creative thoughts branch out. How the writer constructs and organises the text will greatly affect reader blockages one way or another.

Most reading happens under pressure when time is a critical factor. Often there is something equally demanding of the reader's attention. Above all else, the demands of **urgency** upon readers require most of the writer, for holding their attention in the face of stress. It is incumbent upon the writer to aim for least effort on the part of readers in coming to terms with the written product.

Latent Readers

Through the written product, the professional person has rendered a service to the client and interested other parties in line with their expectations. There are, however, expectations of a different kind to be met or surpassed that lie outside those types of readers and the somewhat forensic examination of readership above.

As stated earlier, the professional person writes *for* and on *behalf* of the client, reaching a particular readership. By means of the functions of *gravity, tone* and *expression*, the written product has an inherent significance that lays bare the essence of the professional person (Chapter One ~ see *Inherent Significance*). Being prone in that way, the professional person knows that those readers will hold them to account if mistakes are made and/or the task performed falls below the expected general standards of those within the same profession (Chapter Two ~ see *Conduct*).

Additionally, the written product will reach beyond the overt readership (the client and interested other parties). There will be the peers of the professional person as well as other people, for whatever reason, who will be latent readers. These will be inclined to take the written product as a representative example of the expected general standards of the profession. In that sense, the professional person writes on behalf of the body of members of the profession as a whole to a standard that contributes to a **reference** position.

There will be occasions when overt readers will be tolerant of a limited effort to the writing task, for any number of reasons, such as costs, urgency, expediency, etc. Unaware of, or unfettered by, those reasons, latent readers will not be so tolerant because of the poor professional image. The professional person must be mindful always to at least reach the expected general standards of the profession. An ambassadorial mindset is required.

A summary listing of the parameters of readership appears in Table 3.

Table 3: Parameters of Readership

presence	)	
handling	)	REQUIREMENTS
causation	)	DEMANDS
temperament	)	
alignment	)	INTERESTS
inclination	)	
strategy	)	HABITS
concentration	)	CAPACITY
reference	)	LATENCY

Awareness – Knowing Readers

Readers expect to be able to take the written product of the professional person and comfortably follow where it leads. Readers are a complex body with an eclectic character that firmly burdens the writing task. Coming to grips with readers is essential, and a number of controlling variables, or parameters, help by marking out the potential boundaries of their domain. These embrace such things as the interests, habits and capacity of readers. Being so mindful of the domain of readers greatly assists the writer to communicate reliably with them.

Insight

How written work is read is as important as how it is written. Not all readers will be on the writer's side and many will not be eager recipients of the written product. However, each will expect professionalism in written work, to witness that the writer knows the subject and field in question. Readers will presume that the writer has, through building upon customary literary skill, given full attention to the effort of reading. They will never forgive the writer who demands too much of them, leaving them to stray, out of control, from the intended meaning. The accomplished professional is a good communicator, not least by being efficiently fluent (much more about this in Parts II and III).

Code of Awareness ~ Tranche 3: Task Awareness

The measures to embrace in the writing task
Never overlook comprehensively gauging the readership or communication requirements of the finished written product, to arrange and choose words carefully, as they will certainly be received (eventually) with scrutiny. Decide where and how to focus on readers by embracing the following measures:

- presence – bridge the communication gap through creating a writer-presence to readers and feel their presence continually, so not to write in isolation.
- handling – give guidance to meaning as much as possible when writing, especially for it to continue as long as possible when in the readers' hands, to attune readers appropriately.
- causation – meticulously establish and monitor the causation for the work in question, to verify the scope and detailed tasks.
- temperament – research temperaments to anticipate the relevance to readers of the work in question.
- alignment – seek an alignment with a light touch to leave no readers feeling excluded, and write for the 'losing party' (those most hostile).
- inclination – arrange text to suit the inclination of candidate readers, concerning their preferred reading methods.
- strategy – respond especially to the strategy of

reading that is most appropriate to the content.

- concentration – structure the written product to aid concentration, particularly in the face of the potential blockages to quick understanding they are likely to encounter.
- urgency – make the reading experience trouble-free, swift and pleasant in deference to the urgency the reader brings to the written product.
- reference – go beyond the forensic treatment of readership and be a worthy ambassador for the profession, to meet and surpass the reference position for generally expected standards; see it as a threshold to be crossed.

Do not lose vital passengers along the way.

II. RESPONSIBILITY

JOURNEY HAZARDS

Awareness enlightens responsibility, which is the other attitudinal 'pillar of professionalism'. The professional person has freely accepted responsibility for shaping a fault-free written product. Where there is a breakdown in awareness, the written product becomes faulty with corresponding problems concerning the accuracy, precision and clarity of it. Part II to *Professionalism on the Page* establishes the perception for responsible action, with particular reference to the reasons for faults, when misadventure runs amok.

The terrain of pitfalls of purpose (Chapter Four) and the territory of the minefield of motivation (Chapter Five) each give rise to a tranche or layer to a Code of Responsibility, which feeds the anticipation of fault problems through opportune and confident practices.

Part II is both the terrain and the territory, the hazardous landscape, as it were, through which the route of the writing journey must pass, which is down to the writer-driver to negotiate safely.

PROFESSIONALISM ON THE PAGE

Chapter Four
THE PITFALLS OF PURPOSE

Those things that hurt, instruct.

Benjamin Franklin 1706-1790
American statesman and scientist

Concerns

Those things that hurt the written product are particular faults, or pitfalls, that make it hard or impossible to fulfil the writing purpose to any reasonable standard. Being able to spot these in advance gives an opportunity for pre-emptive attention; they are instructive if fully understood. Not facing up to faults and blindly, inattentively stumbling forward over such terrain, is a sure way of attracting misadventure in the writing task.

> What are the faults that hurt written products? What is it about them that will instruct the writing task?

This chapter assesses faults that surface in the written product to set out practices in response. Again, the use of the bold font gives emphasis to the first mentioning of faults; responsible practices appear at the end of the chapter and are underlined.

Faults reflect the reckless driving behaviour of misadventure with the vehicle of prose.

Faults, Problems and Opportunities

Faults are not peripheral matters for they adversely impinge upon the writing purpose of *conveying best advice with influence* (Chapter One ~ see *Inherent Significance*). Sadly, they have an unremitting prevalence as a great volume of actual written work testifies, from various disciplines and levels of seniority (all the way to the top). This is the written work presented in thousands of guises over many years for examination and testing by this author. In all probability, these faults frequent the workplace of many enterprises; there is no reason to believe otherwise.

Faults occur when there is a breakdown in the writer's command of language, for that is the essence of both communication and thought. Pitfalls are menacing faults that cause havoc through poor fluency that fails to unite the subject matter with readers. Readers are bereft of an efficiently fluent text that is comfortably understandable (Chapter Three ~ see *Awareness – Knowing Readers... Insight*). The writer is bereft of an effectively fluent text that apprises readers of substance (Chapter One ~ see *Awareness – Seeing Word Power... Insight*). The written product must have the capacity of fluency about it: efficiency to serve the reader, effectiveness to serve the writer.

A written product with poor fluency to it leads to serious communication difficulties. Such difficulties result in an inability to execute the business of the day, either in terms of delay when clarification is sought and when unforeseen misinterpretation is corrected, or in terms of total inaction due to confusion, uncertainty or indeed reader fatigue.

Pitfalls are intellectual in nature, arising outside the correctness of English usage, and implicate natural tendencies in extempore conversational speech and poor thinking. They reflect harm done to accuracy, precision or clarity through weaknesses that mostly enfeeble, or through failings that mostly flaw, the written product. Pitfalls impede or jeopardise fulfilling the writing purpose and have no place in considered professional text.

Even with the best of intentions, as the writing task proceeds, problems are likely to surface incrementally because the writer is inclined in some way or other to lose plain sight of the functions of prose, attributes of professionalism and parameters of readership. It is a type of blindness to the many factors involved in these areas that faults develop in the form of problems with accuracy, precision and clarity. There is ignorant inattention to the factors in the Code of Awareness.

Clients and others hold professional people responsible for the content of work, especially when presented in the body of a written product. Being responsive to and answerable for faults therein is very much the lot of the professional person. This requires vigilance, for spotting signs of inattention to certain awareness factors in a timely manner. It is through vigilance that faults become problem-opportunities for pre-emptive attention.

The Code of Awareness has no less than thirty-nine factors (Chapters One, Two & Three, respectively). All factors are responsible for faults in some way or other. Most apply to more than one fault, and it is difficult to differentiate any that do not. However, it is instructive to assign each factor once only to where it is most instrumental to the fault. In the assessment that follows, each fault signals more than one factor instrumental to it, which is the experience of this author. The several instrumental factors shed light on the corresponding problems to each fault.

What follows, though detailed, is not a forensic analysis but a pragmatic assessment stopping short of the complexity where faults overlay one upon another. Given that complexity, others may take a different view about the detail given. In any event, the construction of the assessment, in terms of the key associations between awareness, faults and problems, remains valid for bringing the everyday written work of professional people into the realm of accurate, precise and clear, thoughtful expression.

Weaknesses

In this category of faults, the poor fluency of the writer is mainly evident in the capacity of not connecting content with readers (inefficiency). Here are the five most prevalent types that surface in varying degrees in written products. The assessment reports each weakness fault by type and description and then by an account of the corresponding problems. These are expressed in terms of the harm and image the fault has, with particular reference to the underlying (most instrumental) awareness factors.

The fault of **disorder** presents itself especially in complex work or wherever a comprehensive treatment of the subject is necessary. The text of the written product has a poor focus to it as there is undue attention to inconsequential, peripheral matters. The writer treats these over-generously, with an absence of discerning thought to keep them in their place. It is unclear to the reader where the substantive and determinative matters lie and how the work advances them. Some content is irrelevant and potentially divergent.

The fault of disorder works against the reader's memory. Having a focus in a written product is akin to telling a story. With a story, the writer selects which information to retain and which to lose in line with a chosen perspective that directs readers where to focus. A story fills out a mental picture and exerts power beyond the obvious bits and pieces within, as the unified whole is greater than the sum of the parts. A good story captures the reader's attention.

Disorder harms clarity. A muddled-looking written product has somewhat rambling and hesitant content. The messy writer's *handling* of meaning is poor, with choices of words and their arrangement not benefitting from *contemplation*, being unsuited to steadfastly directing the reader towards interpretation, and frustrating *recollection.*

The fault of **discord** is common and annoying, compounding the above confusion. Meanings become obscure as statements in the written product about much the same thing are varied; the writer restates content capriciously and unreliably. This is commonplace when the writer embellishes content imperfectly, especially with the misuse of synonyms, adjectives, adverbs and abstract nouns. Loose thinking and misunderstanding cause misconstructions, especially when the writer makes little effort to establish and adhere to actual meanings.

Discord harms precision and clarity. A vague-looking written product introduces uncertainty, as there is a lack of firmness, with keywords and important text not standing out. The lazy writer's inadequate prose leaves *capacity* to confuse the reader, making difficult the reading habits of *inclination* and *strategy.*

The fault of **ostentation** is, sadly, about verbosity, pretentiousness and pomposity that bring confusion of a different kind. Much of the text of the so afflicted written product becomes unmanageable through 'overwriting' as if speaking to the reader, an indulgence that is tolerated because key readers are more or less obliged to continue reading. There is too much description for the eye to take in, usually with long words and over-complex sentences. Knowledge-inappropriate language is used, notably jargon. At best, the writer misunderstands how to impart content impressively; at worst, the writer's breathtaking self-indulgence unwittingly excludes readers from what is self-obsessed, off-putting work.

Ostentation harms precision and clarity. An elaborate-looking written product has long, drawn-out swathes of meaningless words. The self-indulgent writer of the cumbrous text of this kind causes reader *concentration* and *urgency* to flounder.

The fault of **voracity** is another related to elaboration. The overeager writer will saturate the text with extraordinary information and personal knowledge about the work in question. Additional material may be relevant, to a point, and carry weight on the first impression, but often it amounts to needless elaboration with insignificant text that overwhelms readers. The writer seizes the opportunity to share understanding and impress the reader, often because of a passion for the subject.

Voracity harms clarity. With it, an overloaded-looking written product is frustrating for the reader, as more detail is set down than is necessary. The extravagant writer overlooks the *temperament* of readers and does not think about the *alignment* of content.

The fault of **escalation**, not unlike voracity and ostentation, adds tiresome length to the text of the written product when the writer believes consolidation and fortification of content to be necessary. It occurs with the writer attempting to reinforce or bolster, layer upon layer, critical arguments with others that happen to be loosely connected or not particularly relevant. Escalation is counterproductive when ultimately the text fails to be carefully scrutinised. Even so, the writer feels unable to rely upon frankness about modest or clear-cut results and as a precaution seeks to influence the reader further at all costs.

Escalation harms accuracy and clarity. With it, a blurred-looking written product suggests a 'smokescreen' in operation for concealment of the simplest truth of the matter. The guarded writer produces a largely complicated, dense text through limited *practical intelligence* and *integrity*, with the *presence* of readers hesitantly in mind.

Table 4(a) gives a summary of the assessment of weaknesses.

Table 4(a): Pitfalls of Purpose ~ Weaknesses

Fault	Problem(s)	Factor(s)
disorder (muddled)	clarity	handling/contemplation/recollection
discord (vague)	precision/clarity	capacity/inclination/strategy
ostentation (elaborate)	precision/clarity	concentration/urgency
voracity (overloaded)	clarity	temperament/alignment
escalation (blurred)	accuracy/clarity	presence/practical-intelligence/integrity

Failings

In this category of faults, the poor fluency of the writer is mainly evident in the capacity of not projecting substance (ineffectiveness). As before with weaknesses, here are the five most prevalent types of failings that surface in varying degrees in written products. The same structure of assessment is given, reporting each failure fault by type, description and corresponding problems, with the underlying instrumental factors shown.

The fault of **laxity** is most notable where the environment of the written work of others is poor, owing to the dominance of transmitted words in casual, informal exchanges that cross over. The writer is unduly influenced by that writing environment and 'runs with the herd', following too closely the informality or practice of others. It is a 'that will do' syndrome. Any meaningful effort is largely surrendered by the writer alongside an abrogation of responsibility *to convey best advice with influence* (Chapter One ~ see *Inherent Significance*). The customary literary skill of a professional person is hard to see in the written product, which is unimpressive. Literary skill should always impress and set the professional person apart.

Laxity harms accuracy, precision and clarity. With it, an inferior-looking written product fails to carry influence. The *ease* and *licence* of transmitted words have taken over by virtue of an inappropriate *tone*, and there is the absence of *authority* and *legitimacy*, the whole reflecting badly upon the *expression* of intellect and identity. A written product so afflicted poorly serves the *reference* standard and is potentially damaging. Generally, the irresolute writer makes little effort to communicate in a considerate way through professional *courtesy*.

The fault of **distortion** has echoes of voracity but takes the discordant text to unsafe levels through interfering with the articulation of inputs, which are thereby at risk of becoming corrupted. Inputs to written work are all those things arrived at for stating at the outset because they will be either agreed or undisputed information, factual or otherwise. Where there is room for manoeuvre, many errant writers are fond of presenting these in their own terms. They regurgitate them unnecessarily for various reasons, namely: to give emphasis; to impose a style; to demonstrate understanding; and, mistakenly, to advance the work. Ignorantly or disingenuously, the writer mistreats inputs, which become misconstrued and misleading.

Inputs are not the intellectual property of the writer and must only ever be amended where they are patently misleading or inaccurately expressed, and then the 'what, why and how' of it must be reported fully. Any amendments for clarification or correction require great care and consistency.

Distortion harms accuracy and precision. With it, a misleading-looking written product has traceable misrepresentations, with signs of unnecessary interference or questionable tampering. The *versatility* of prose leads the meddlesome writer of limited *competence* astray, with the *force* of prose becoming misdirected.

The fault of **incongruity** also involves the mistreatment of inputs, but concerns particularly the subsequent constructions. The writer does not prudently address matters that are insubstantial or contradictory. Often this is when there is an abundance of information. The writer neglects to assign appropriate weight to inputs, leaving open the door to logic or probabilities flawed by fallacies and bias or other falsehoods. Incongruity occurs particularly when incorrect arguments flourish for a number of reasons, namely: there is a popular viewpoint in support; there is anecdotal (unrepresentative) evidence; there is endorsement by an 'authority' figure or body; supporting evidence is selective; there is repetition giving the illusion of weighty matters; finally, there are euphemisms and jargon that obscure. In short, the writer is unable to see the wood for the trees.

Incongruity harms accuracy. With it, an unsound-looking written product becomes challengeable because of somewhat disproportionate, inconsistent and conflicting elements to the text. The neglectful writer fails to exhaust *critical thinking* and obtain authentic results, which jeopardises the function of *validation*.

The fault of **incoherence,** unlike incongruity with its abundant information, arises when the writer does not harness sufficient material to fully support the arguments presented. Particularly, a seamless presentation of these is absent because of insufficient knowledge or information and there is a breakdown in connective thought.

The writer makes 'creative leaps' in response to the insufficient material without 'back-reasoning' or bridging assumptions. Creative leaps are damaging unless they are capable of representation as acceptable assumptions that support them. Alternatively, if they are the product of intuitive thought, backward appraisal to establish continuity is required.

Incoherence harms accuracy and precision. With it, a fragile-looking written product has poor connectivity through the insufficient material. The reckless writer relies upon limited *temporal knowledge* and inappropriate use of creative leaps in the absence of *instinctual knowledge* and sound *reasoning*.

The fault of **misconstruction** occurs even when there is sufficient material harnessed to support fully the arguments presented. With this fault, there is an unsatisfactory relationship between the start and the finish of the written product. It amounts to a breakdown within the body of the work whereby the finish is incapable of being a conclusive or helpful product of its start. There is a static starting position, notwithstanding what unfolds later in the work. Lines of enquiry do not inform the starting position and go on to reach their natural conclusion irrespectively. The writer looks ahead, without backward checks, and the finish becomes adrift of its source.

The start to the writing task sets out the matters for attention in order to reach a finish in fulfilment of the work purpose. The finish is implicit in the start. If the writer poorly communicates the starting position, the finish cannot do justice to it and even if it has helpful manifestation there is the risk of so-called 'mission creep', an expansion or more likely a divergence, where the finish is off course. There should be no doubt whatsoever where the written product is to head, and its finish must square with that. It is a vital form of closure, as with all storytelling.

Misconstruction harms precision. With it, an unstable-looking written product fails to fulfil the work purpose. The careless writer follows a largely uncharted and undeveloped framework of *causation*, which shrouds the reader/client demands, and the writing task flounders because of a lack of *diligence*.

Table 4(b) gives a summary of the assessment of failings.

Table 4(b): Pitfalls of Purpose
~ Failings

Fault	Problem(s)	Factor(s)
laxity (inferior)	accuracy/precision/ clarity	ease/licence/tone/ authority/legitimacy/ expression/reference/ courtesy
distortion (misleading)	accuracy/precision	versatility/competence/ force
incongruity (unsound)	accuracy	critical thinking/ validation
incoherence (fragile)	accuracy/precision	temporal knowledge/ instinctual knowledge/ reasoning
misconstruction (unstable)	precision	causation/diligence

The Terrain of Pitfalls

The two tables 4(a) & 4(b) above show intellectual faults that comprise the terrain of pitfalls to the writing task, as associated with an inarticulate (non-fluent) writer.

Responsibility – Confronting Weaknesses and Failings

Unresolved faults in the written product damage the writing purpose by virtue of problems with accuracy, precision and clarity. Faults have different levels of severity, namely weaknesses and failings, attributable to poor language fluency. They show themselves in different ways, from muddled text to unstable content. The corresponding problems (above) arise because awareness about what shapes the written product is wanting; the writer does not see instrumental factors concerning the functions of prose, the attributes of professionalism and the parameters of readership. Instrumental factors alert the writer to appropriate attention in the writing task.

Insight

Clients and others are entitled to expect professional people to bring a fully developed awareness to the writing table, from which to apply freely accepted responsibility for a fault-free, fluent product. Being able to recognise and understand faults is imperative to the writing task. Knowing how, why and when faults come about, particularly to see what is going through the mind of the errant writer, points the way for a considered response in the writing task. Know the fault to know the writer not to be. The accomplished professional is ever vigilant and rigorously anticipates faults in the exercise of freely accepted responsibility.

Code of Responsibility ~ Tranche 1: Intellectual Responsibility

The vigilance to bring to the writing task

It is hard to be vigilant. A person will see what they are conditioned to expect to see. As inattention to the instrumental factors (shown in *italics*) is likely to strike as faults, call upon vigilance for an opportune response. Anticipate the fault problems with efficiently and effectively fluent text, by engaging in these opportune practices:

Weaknesses – *Inefficient Fluency*

- muddled through disorder by the messy writer – have a mental picture of the 'story' to tell for a clear focus (recollection), reflecting on the gist of the text as it unfolds, before finally setting it down and judiciously closing off peripheral matters (contemplation and handling). This is the practice of <u>unfolding the message</u>.
- vague through discord by the lazy writer – choose words and their arrangement consistently, correctly and wisely in the face of the potential for confusion and criticism (capacity), using them astutely at all times for aiding reading habits (inclination and strategy). This is the practice of <u>rationalising meaning</u>.
- elaborate through ostentation by the self-indulgent writer – see and hear words and their arrangement

through the reader's 'eye-voice', as a novelist would, not through the 'thought voice' of the writer's speech (concentration), respecting the investment in the written product of precious reading time that is not to be wasted (urgency). This is the practice of <u>envisaging text</u>.

- overloaded through voracity by the extravagant writer – spot extravagances that are unhelpful to the simplicity of 'need to know' information fully in tune with readers' interests (temperament), realising that readers will be thankful immediately to be able to seize upon what matters to them, free of needless elaboration (alignment). This is the practice of <u>streamlining content</u>.
- blurred through escalation by the guarded writer – stand confidently behind disappointing results (practical intelligence), resisting the natural temptation to bolster things with spurious or unnecessary content (integrity), mindful always of the need to narrow the communication gap between writer and reader (presence). This is the practice of frankly <u>upholding bare results</u>.

Failings – *Ineffective Fluency*

- inferior through laxity by the irresolute writer – intend always to be set apart from everyday average abilities, showing literary skill devoid of casual prose (ease, licence and tone), articulating the customary traditional stature of a professional person (authority and legitimacy) and providing a worthy standard (reference), befitting both intellect and professional identity (expression). Write deferentially to impress the reader, making words and their arrangement attractive, meaningful, manageable and relevant (courtesy). This is the practice of <u>showcasing stature</u>.

- misleading through distortion by the meddlesome writer – make any clarifications to inputs with great care and consistency (versatility), refraining from needless and misguided amendments (competence) for faithful influential content (force). This is the practice of <u>manifesting facts</u> ('hard' and 'soft', including the intellectual property of others). That said, there are occasions for challenging inputs (next).

- unsound through incongruity by the neglectful writer – probe and investigate the face value of inputs (critical thinking), dealing with the insubstantial or contradictory ones, dismissing any that do not cross the respective factual or probability thresholds and organising all survivors by the weight they carry (validation). This is the practice of <u>testing knowledge</u>.

- fragile through incoherence by the reckless writer – leave no gaps in reasoning, exploring parallel lines of argument in response, engaging in further research for better temporal knowledge and translating any disruptions into 'bridging assumptions', aided by instinctual knowledge, for checking with back-reasoning. This is the practice of <u>advancing the case</u>.

- unstable through misconstruction by the careless writer – keep the start-finish ends to the writing task in plain view and under review at all times, taking periodic and routine visits back to the start, developing or revising issues and objects (causation) and expressing them unequivocally through progressive refinement, for accurate thinking and where that leads (diligence). This is the practice of <u>moderating context</u>.

Intellectual faults do not account for all the awareness factors. 'Mood faults', dealt with in the next chapter, account for the rest.

Be ready to detect and steer clear of pitfalls.

Chapter Five
THE MINEFIELD OF MOTIVATION

Nothing in life is to be feared; it is only to be understood.

Marie Curie (1867-1934)
Polish-born French Nobel Prize-winning chemist

Concerns

To the intellectual faults arising from blindly stumbling along the writing journey (pitfalls) must be added others of a different nature that are attributable to the state of mind, or mood, of the writer, namely: mood faults. The territory or battleground of office life, whether central or peripheral to the professional person, is a veritable mood minefield that professionals ignore at their peril. Many fall victim to fears therein and go forward reluctantly in the writing task, occasioning faults at the outset.

> What fears affect the state of mind of the professional person? What faults in the written product arise and what do these mean for the writing task?

This chapter assesses mood faults to set out practices in response. As with the previous chapter, the use of the bold font gives emphasis to the first mentioning of faults; responsible practices appear at the end and are underlined.

Mood faults signify feeble driving behaviour with the vehicle of prose.

Fear, Mood and Motivation

The professional person does not work in isolation. There is a complex, troublesome environment of people, a workplace of connections, including that in which the work in question has originated and that through which it is to be manifest. Undaunted, the professional person must move the writing task in hand firmly in the right direction by summoning a positive outlook and a purposeful intent (Chapter Two ~ see *Awareness – Understanding Stature… Insight*). The professional person must come to understand that the role of negative forces is an integral part of the writing task, upon which reliability largely depends.

Potentially uncontrollable or unavoidable workplace events stimulate fear in the professional person by virtue of real or perceived threats to their status, power and security. For the writing task, these real or perceived threats come about because of the unknown (where is this task leading? – what lies ahead?), uncertainty (how is it to be done? – what inputs are called for?) and unpredictability (how will it be done? – what participation will be given to it?). The looming large of such difficulties produces an unpleasant state of inner turmoil that is stressful. This is the mood of anxiety, which is closely associated with fear of failure and fear of difficult people. It is responsible for mood faults in written work, with recognisable corresponding problems concerning accuracy, precision and clarity.

Moods act as demotivators. The professional person has authentic motivation through self-belief and other attributes (Chapter Two ~ see *Personality*). However, with the mood of anxiety, coping with the future or imminent difficulties of the task in hand causes the mustering of self-belief to be a struggle. In any event, within the workplace, whether of private practice, bureaucracy or business organisation, the demands of multitasking, priorities, urgency and profitability are likely to impose time constraints that make matters worse.

Additionally, unsupportive colleagues greatly test the self-belief of the professional person. They do so in terms of their behaviour towards the writer, the written product or the writing task itself. They are often feared because of the difficulties they present. There are those with pessimistic, off-putting attitudes who share their bleak thoughts (fuelling the unknown), those who criticise whatever is done (fuelling the uncertain), and those who withhold information (fuelling the unpredictable). Surprisingly and worryingly, there are those who seek to undermine constructive effort by any means.

Not knowing the harmful intentions behind certain unsupportive colleagues compounds the stress and dread of dealing with them. They variously lack empathy and seek to ingratiate, looking for admiration, attention and high status. Their behaviour is to exploit, deceive, manipulate and take for granted work colleagues. In some quarters, notably in the focus of Oliver James' book *Office Politics,* they have been dramatically termed 'toxic people' of a psychopathic (emotionally unstable and cold), Machiavellian (cunning and deceitful) or narcissistic (self-admiring) disposition.

If that is not enough to cope with, then there are those colleagues who do not measure up in the way required of them; they are 'imposters' acting out a role with superficiality. Having to work with or through such people adds to the anxiety-induced stress or difficulty of the task in hand because support of any consequence is not there when needed.

Mood Management and Coping Strategies

Moods can be overwhelming for they strike at any time for any number of reasons, biochemical or psychological. Even so, they are valuable indicators about our feelings. Moods mask true feelings, each being a transitory, internal subjective emotional state. The psychology to rid oneself of unpleasant emotions is complex. This author acknowledges that bringing gripping, personal moods under control is well beyond most of us without expert guidance. At the typical everyday work level, however, when a grey mood of anxiety prevails, the writer feels rather threatened and demotivated and applies ways of coping.

Understanding the attendant fear becomes a type of essential feedback that improves self-knowledge. Mood management is about becoming less self-preoccupied, not to be at the mercy of workplace moods and wallow in a vulnerable state, but to commit to some course of action. Being purposeful with as much positive outlook as possible to communicate is what successful people do: they manage, if not control, their workplace moods best. In that regard, the authentic motivation of professional people greatly helps.

When that motivation falters and responsible mood management is absent, in the mood of anxiety a stressed writer is likely to react with default coping strategies of one form or another. These palliative, short-term, negative practices are very much at odds with a professional treatment of the task in hand and give rise to faulty written work.

Coping strategies that involve certain practices are likely to cause a leaning towards untroublesome effort in the writing task. They are maladaptive in that they do not improve functioning but merely reduce symptoms. Of particular relevance are these two: <u>avoidance</u> / <u>escape</u> of anxiety-provoking situations, or a reliance on <u>safety</u> measures of some kind. With the coping strategies of 'avoidance' or 'safety' in place, a type of *comfort bias* is inflicted upon the written product, wherein the writer has drawn towards an untroublesome comfort zone of mixed content. With the coping strategy of escape, a type of *token effort bias* is inflicted, wherein the writer has drawn towards minimal, inescapable content only.

(More about these later.)

At times, the writer experiences anxiety with depression: a feeling of hopelessness or worthlessness. Serious psychiatric syndromes aside, in the context of *Professionalism on the Page*, the so-called depressed writer is one who is at least despondent and most likely discouraged and disillusioned, notably a person with low morale. Depression of this sort is a normal reaction to workplace problems that pose perceived insurmountable difficulties. For the professional person with a challenging writing task, these difficulties will be associated with the 'fear of failure' and 'the fear of toxic colleagues'.

In that minefield of fears will be the major source of stress of a 'to do' list, with which comes a sense of foreboding. Uncertainty and indecision about the 'must do', 'should do' and 'could do' tasks make taking action difficult and a feeling of helplessness prevails. Anxiety-linked depression fosters low energy and aversion to activity.

Where fear of one kind or another in the mind of the writer has affronted motivation, the attractiveness of either the comfort bias or the token bias will compete with the demands of the functions of prose, attributes of professionalism and parameters of readership. Certain of these demands upon the writer are likely to suffer from a lack of mood management, allowing the painless path to dominate the writing task (Chapter Seven ~ see *Positive Purposefulness*). This is reluctance and personal convenience: an expediency of circumstance.

It is wholly unsatisfactory to let moods be, as the originating pressures of stress and conflict are mostly transitory, whereas the responsibilities of professionalism are enduring.

Unintended Consequences

Coping with the unknown, the uncertain and the unpredictable is not only to do with the workplace environment and fearful anxiety. Troubled motivation is also due to a fear of triggering the wrong outcomes by failing to get things right. This is fear of the unexpected, which produces the mood of unease in the form of an inclination towards the lack of confidence and self-doubt (Chapter Two ~ see *Conduct*).

An unexpected wrong outcome is endemic in public policymaking and there are breathtaking examples. The '*cobra effect*' (in one form or another) is a term often used. This stems from India when a policy to reduce the snake population comprised offering a bounty for every skin of a captured cobra. In the event, those who took to breeding, raising and slaughtering the species for gain claimed much of the bounty. The cobra policy unintentionally led to a substantial snake-breeding industry and did little to reduce the wild population.

The cobra effect relates to the 'Law of Unintended Consequences'. This idiomatic term conveys the difficulties in getting things right overall, especially where complexity and understanding are problematic. Under this 'law', unforeseen outcomes (drawbacks and perverse results, but benefits, too) can be actuated by well-meaning intentions that have not been exhaustively appraised. Unintended consequences are not peripheral matters. Not only are actions of government very much about managing unintended consequences, the risk of unexpected outcomes is a significant concern in professional life, too.

Unexpected outcomes can arise for various reasons. Firstly, the work of the professional person, if not subjective or dependent upon circumstance, is often innovative, turning in unfamiliar and problematic directions. Where work such as this necessitates ingenuity, there is seldom a 'right answer'. Secondly, there is the long reach work areas have, affecting many unknown situations. Lastly, there are the significant outcomes for people that are at stake, notably in recommending a decision or a standpoint, or in deciding a scheme or a course of action (Chapter One ~ see *Inherent Significance*). The so-called unintended consequences, the unexpected wrong outcomes of a flawed written product, are potentially serious, even when not spectacular. All manner of curative or corrective efforts usually follow at considerable expense.

A reluctance to immerse oneself fully in the work subject is behind much of it because there is a failure to get at root causes to the problem matters under examination with the work in question. The written product must raise and address the right questions. Raising the wrong question will yield the wrong answer.

For example, when heating bills are too high the question often asked is 'how to conserve heat better?'

With well-insulated homes, this question leads to fruitless results. A different question is 'how to make heating appliances more fuel-efficient?' There is the one problem of how to reduce consumption and bills, but two questions defining it. Knowing the right question to ask in the circumstances is the key.

Asking the right question is not a straightforward matter, as we tend to gravitate towards the obvious when the root cause is hidden somewhere else. In the example above, the root cause of high bills may well be a lifestyle and behavioural matters concerning the careless comings and goings of occupants or their preferences for insubstantial fashionable clothing. A behavioural-type question would then become the key to solving the problem.

In many matters also, readers have a heavy investment in their opinion and feel confident they are right; they are difficult to influence otherwise. This is especially the case when they run with the 'herd' or tide of opinion. When the reader is so poorly served by the written product, the message contained therein is easily misconstrued and acted upon in a manner that was unintended by the writer. Alternatively, subject to how the reader is disposed towards the written product (Chapter Three ~ see 'temperament'), unexpected challenges in various forms will result. Readers will look for signs to seek out information or evidence that confirms what they already think. Rightly or wrongly, these tendencies bring into question the message and lessen its intended influence.

Mood Faults

A minefield, in this context, is a place that threatens to blow the writing task off course through the writer's poor resilience to moods, succumbing to reluctant and inadequate effort. The writer thereby inflicts one or more mood faults upon the written product. Mood faults reflect poor mood management: the want of a positive outlook with purposeful intent. Unlike intellectual faults, which are matters of pure mental acuity that surface during the course and challenges of the writing task, mood faults are the result of the writer's mental health concerning motivational struggles at the outset and they have a common effect.

As with intellectual faults, the sources to these mood faults are traceable to factors within the Code of Awareness. These factors indicate opportunities for mood management. Of the thirty-nine factors in the Code, thirty-one are most instrumental to intellectual faults. Following the approach of that assessment, each of the eight factors remaining is most instrumental to a particular mood fault, appearing once only and set (amongst others) against the fault in question. As before, the experience of this author informs the assessment.

Faults of the Comfort Bias

With the coping strategy of avoidance in place, the writer avoids fear by following the path of least resistance. An unduly circumscribed written product has the fault of **partiality**. With the reluctance to tackle difficult people head-on, or to deal with the circumstances associated therewith, comes the inadequate pursuit of all lines of investigation and argument, in subject or depth. The written product has a bias not only because of its orientation, but also because of inputs tainted by insufficient testing.

Partiality is different to the intellectual fault of incongruity, where inputs are mishandled through inattention (Chapter Four ~ see *Failings*) because here they become tainted due to the reluctance to investigate fully.

Partiality harms accuracy. With it, an uneven-looking written product has misleading results, either by content or by weight. The reserved writer allows truncated and deflected lines of investigation to occur and gives undue emphasis to easier avenues, as personal standards are let slip with hesitant *conscientiousness*. The truth of the matter is uncertain, bringing into question *honesty*.

With the coping strategy of safety in place, the writer shelters from fear by pursuing secure lines of investigation and argument only. The writer has a **fixation** to keep to habitually trusted knowledge and practices, and fails to ask all the right questions, for fear that some may lead to the territory of difficult people or circumstances. Believing they know more than they know sustains this fault. Essentially, such a writer is playing safe and stays comfortably within the familiar due to the threat of feelings of insecurity. Usefully, if not creatively, the writer interprets the client's brief or task instructions to suit. The writer is often fixated in a single-minded way on certain outcomes.

Fixation harms accuracy. With it, a seductive-looking written product gives a thorough and detailed treatment of a particular view of the work in question, but a confined picture of the truth of the matter as a whole. There is inadequate coverage and content. The insecure writer applies a narrow view and gives insufficient weight to the *gravity* of the work in question, as well as to the *impact* of the results obtained.

Faults of the Token Bias

With the coping strategy of escape in place, the writer uses **distraction** in one or other forms in order to flee the full burden of responsibility of coming to terms with difficult people or circumstances and new thinking. The writer handles responsibility by limiting expectations of the task in hand, either by allowing more manageable other tasks to get in the way, or by allowing a cloak of jargon to conceal a less than thorough performance, or both.

The aim is to give minimal, inescapable effort to the task in hand but is very different to the intellectual fault of laxity, which is about comfortably fitting in with the prevailing standard (Chapter Four ~ see *Failings*). The token effort through distraction is opposite to the task fault of escalation (building layers of the argument for reinforcement), which concerns guarded cautiousness; distraction concerns deceit.

Jargon, if not scientific, can be harmful if the intention is not to seek precision but to foster evasion through confusion. The use of jargon in the fault of distraction is prompted differently to that in the faults of ostentation (elaborate) and escalation (blurred) (Chapter Four ~ see *Weaknesses*). As with those cases, however, it involves creating an illusion through camouflage of work that is less substantial than presented.

Distraction harms accuracy, precision and clarity. With it, an impenetrable-looking written product has superficial, flimsy content beneath. The deceitful writer, in effect, abrogates responsibility, which indicates that *emotional intelligence* is under duress and *resilience* to setbacks absent. The mustering of mental acuity falters when the writer's *composure* is lost in the struggle for self-belief.

Faults of the Cobra Effect

When confronted by fear of the unexpected, of triggering the wrong outcome, the writer avoids commitment to a single, outright conclusion. The fault of **prevarication** occurs, whereby there is an unrequited responsibility to give best advice firmly, with influence. There is a preference to keep open all possibilities and outcomes, to 'hedge one's bets' so to speak. There is an evenness to alternate lines of investigation and argument in the written product, which has a bias towards subject neutrality.

Prevarication is different to the fault of distraction. Whereas there is an abrogation of responsibility in both cases, it is by different means for different reasons. Unlike distraction, prevarication need not obviate thorough work. Prevarication is similar to the fault of fixation above, when it is a means of 'playing safe' with potentially difficult issues as against a potentially difficult workplace.

Prevarication harms accuracy and precision. With it, a finely poised-looking written product has unhelpful results because there is neither incisiveness nor decisiveness to it. An unduly overcautious writer is uneasy about being able to get at the truth of the situation through exhaustive appraisal of root causes. *Objectivity* suffers because there is poor synthesis to an appraisal that gives matters equal attention, even where they have disproportionate worth.

Table 5 gives a summary of the assessment of mood faults.

Table 5: Minefield of Motivation

Fault	*Problem(s)*	*Factor(s)*
partiality (uneven)	accuracy	conscientiousness/ honesty
fixation (seductive)	accuracy	gravity/impact
distraction (impenetrable)	accuracy/ precision/clarity	emotional intelligence/ resilience/composure
prevarication (poised)	accuracy/ precision	objectivity

The Territory of the Minefield

Table 5 above shows mood faults that comprise the territory of the minefield to the writing journey, as associated with a mood-impaired writer. These compound the potential for misadventure from intellectual faults that comprise the terrain of pitfalls (Chapter Four ~ see *Tables 4a & 4b*).

Responsibility – Opposing Negative Forces

The professional person has ever-present fears. Temporary mood faults are associated with fear-driven anxiety about failing in the task in hand and about dealing with difficult people. The usual response to anxiety is in the form of certain coping strategies that are maladaptive. Putting reluctant effort into the writing task compromises the writing purpose, by neglect of the functions of prose, the attributes of professionalism and the parameters of readership. Particularly, the professional person with low morale has troubled authentic motivation and uses a 'comfort zone' or 'token effort'. These give rise to a written product faulted by the bias of one form or another and having the recognisable defects of uneven, seductive or impenetrable content. Additionally, the unease of the writer with fearful concerns about unexpected wrong outcomes makes for an unhelpfully poised written product.

Insight
Unlike task faults, which reflect blunders, mood faults reflect a risk aversion that enfeebles the writer's approach. When unhelpful moods strike, the writer has an awareness of what needs to be done (see Part I) but at the same time has reluctance about doing it. Reluctance is irresponsible and a dynamic, 'positive purposefulness' must replace it, in one way or another. The accomplished professional has mood resilience, a confident fortitude to write with inscrutable conduct, unsullied by bias.

Code of Responsibility ~ Tranche 2: Motivational Responsibility

The fortitude to bring to the writing task

Keep foremost in mind the origins of fear, moods and motivation. Resist becoming a victim of inappropriate forms of mood management, recognising telltale faults and the corresponding problems concerning accuracy, precision and clarity. When unhelpful moods are likely to strike as faults, call upon an awareness of the instrumental factors (shown in *italics*) to muster a steadfast response. Have a positive outlook to communicate with purposeful intent by engaging in these confident practices:

- uneven through partiality by the reserved writer – stay professional in all respects and let no excuses dictate otherwise (conscientiousness). Separate the problem from the person. Study obstacles and hindrances from all angles to get at what lies past these. Be definitive and forceful about the minimum acceptable levels of such material for the task in hand, for the written product to satisfy expectations and scrutiny (honesty). This is the practice of <u>tackling impediments</u>.
- seductive through fixation by the insecure writer – make an effort to see above and beyond the parapet to the comfort zone of the familiar. Ask the right questions always and do not imagine or pretend to know the right answers. Expect and be prepared boldly to fail and quit graciously the

lines of investigation and argument that become unproductive, in the interests of establishing the true and best result. Let the questions direct the quest, in deference to what readers need and expect (gravity and impact). This is the practice of <u>discovering substance</u>.

- impenetrable through distraction by the deceitful writer – use the negative forces behind aversion to activity and involvement as a source of information and feedback for self-knowledge and improvement, to become self-assured with a considered and collected manner (composure). Never doubt that the written product will come to be scrutinised at some point when readers and peers penetrate its cloak of jargon and see its impotent core for what it is. See the importance of the contribution the written product, however small, will make to one's personal professional stature and the standing of the profession, aiming always to prove capable (emotional intelligence). Know what is required and do it earnestly, compelled by having a firm approach in mind with clear, unavoidable steps to muster content (resilience). This is the practice of <u>activating potency</u>.

- poised through prevarication by the overcautious writer – refrain from giving equal weight and attention to unequal matters to please everybody. In other words, avoid 'sitting on the fence', such as with '...on the one hand X, but on the other Y...'. Come off the fence by getting to grips as far as possible with root causes. Subject neutrality is not dispassionate impartiality (objectivity). Rigorously distinguish between matters for inescapable conclusions. This is the practice of <u>championing positive results</u>.

Do not let the fuel of motivation run low.

III. PERFORMANCE

SECURE TRAVEL

Having an awareness and being granted freely accepted responsibility orientate the writer to act in a responsive and answerable way. The writer pursues responsible practices concerning vigilance and fortitude, in anticipation of otherwise faulty work (Part II). Part III of *Professionalism on the Page* establishes the proficiency and expertise needed for accomplished performance.

The establishment of a performance aim invites a structured approach, in the form of a conceptual, metaphorical model of the writing journey, to put the writer fully in control in a disciplined, thoughtful way (Chapter Six). With the support of various practical techniques the writer is well placed to convert thought into action (Chapter Seven). These chapters launch the device of *Exact Writing*.

Part III is the way the writer-driver responds to the challenges of the writing journey to successfully reach its destination. It amounts to good driver conduct in charting a route and navigating it productively.

Chapter Six
THE ROUTE OF
SATISFACTION

When goals go, meaning goes.
When meaning goes, purpose goes.
When purpose goes,
Life goes dead on our hands.

Carl Jung 1875-1961
Swiss psychiatrist

Concerns

Many professionals write substantively in terms of the technical demands of the topic in question, marginalising operative thoughts about how best to perform the writing task. They haphazardly perform with no clear sight of a goal or purposeful effort. In their hands, the lifeblood of the writing task is at peril, as they leave it to the insecurities of inclination and good fortune.

What purposeful direction is the writing task to take? How is the lifeblood of the writing task secured? What is the way of *Exact Writing*?

This chapter establishes a performance aim and a method of approach for the writing task, showing the writer the way forward in the writing journey. The use of the bold font gives emphasis to the first mentioning of operative modes to the method.

The way forward is that route of the writing journey over which the driver has the best chance of reaching the intended destination unharmed.

Goals, Meaning and Purpose

To recap, written work of the professional person is considerably meaningful in many respects. With the written product, the professional person expects to communicate influential best advice, in the form of conclusions, decisions, recommendations and the like. Through literary skill, the attributes of professionalism are manifest. At least a workmanlike performance through objective, dispassionate impartiality is vital.

Readers find themselves left to reactivate the meaning of written words as closely as possible to what the writer intended. In all likelihood, readers will be inclined to do this imperfectly for a number of reasons. Featuring prominently amongst those reasons is the writer's misadventure in accuracy, precision and clarity through serious or other blunders (pitfalls) and through risk aversion (minefield) that fault written work. The professional person recognises faults with the benefit of codes of awareness and responsibility.

A message that is falteringly conveyed attracts misgivings about its substance and the influence it carries suffers, potentially compromising the writing purpose. The writing purpose is *to convey best advice with influence*, which is the generic goal of the writing task or, in other words, the destination of the writing journey (Chapter One ~ see *Inherent Significance*).

Many professional people believe they take responsibility for fault-free written work but rely merely upon subject expertise; they attend to the substantive requirements of the subject matter to the writing purpose. There is little heed of readers' requirements and how to exercise influence, for there is a misplaced confidence. Such professionals assume that readers will be captive, obliged to continue reading, and able to grasp enough of what they need to be sufficiently influenced.

In practice, with a default written product of this type, seldom is the pinnacle of best advice attained and much is demanded of readers in any event to follow it (Chapter Three ~ see *Awareness – Knowing Readers*). It amounts to leaving readers to their own devices, letting them make of it what they will and experience the influence it ought to have by chance. This is not the responsible way of a truly professional person. There is a cost to the task in hand, the stature of the writer and the standing of the profession.

It is inescapably a fact that the writer is unable to reach satisfactorily the goal-purpose of the writing task with subject expertise alone; look no further than the Hutton example for evidence of that (Chapter One ~ see *Inherent Significance*). Addressing the mechanisms of the writing task itself for implementation of the Code of Responsibility, with all that it calls upon, is crucial.

The Goal of Customer Satisfaction

In pursuing the goal-purpose of the writing task, the writer can regard readers as 'customers' comprising the client and others, for it is useful to relate most activities to a business representation, which is a popular device nowadays.

Businesses are customer-driven organisations. Every time there is a connection with a customer, an opportunity presents itself to enhance the reputation of the business. A business performs well when customers are satisfied and it is thereby essential for it to manage customer satisfaction. This focusses employees on the importance of fulfilling customer expectations, to attain customer satisfaction. The outlook of staff towards the functioning of the organisation, particularly their role within it, greatly affects performance.

The writer of professional documents is akin to a sole member of staff with the key role in the functioning of the business that is the writing task. The core product is influential best advice and the paramount customer-reader is the client, for the professional person is duty-bound to serve clients' best interests. Even so, to act in the client's best interests largely requires the involvement of other parties, or customer-readers, to whom the professional person must appeal (Chapter Three ~ see *Clients' Demands*).

The writer connects with readers in a virtual moment of opportunity for enhancement of the written product through literary skill, from which reputation and influence flow. It is a moment for fulfilling reader expectations (Chapter Three ~ see *Readers' Interests*).

However, an unbridled business approach is liable to invite counterproductive business-speaking language. This is deliberately vague language. It is a language that is implemented, in the sense that words are chosen for effect rather than meaning. It uses stock phrases or leaden clichés and is not a product of accurate, precise and clear, thoughtful expression. Here is an example of that, another 'find' in John Humphrys' book (*Lost for Words*); it is an attempt to promote discounted seats in a theatre:

We are a global business and we regard ourselves as world-leading and world-beating. .... we are really engaging with both institutions to provide a to-die-for, incredible deal for the consumer. It is much more pro-active than just sticking your name above a production.

A judicious business representation of the writing task, one that does not permit lapses or recourse to 'business-speak', usefully establishes the destination of the goal-purpose of the writing task to be the product of a process of performance.

Successful Performance: The Aim

Success, the *Oxford English Dictionary* tells us, is the accomplishment of an aim. The writer writes for a purpose – the goal destination – and aims to do so as well as possible, for a fault-free written product. To that end and with reference to the intellectual and mood faults assessed in the preceding chapters, the professional person is obliged to write responsibly in accord with many factors: the thirty-nine factors of awareness that, through neglectful inattention, become instrumental to faults.

When conversant with the codes of awareness and responsibility, the professional person fully understands that obligation. With greater understanding comes greater indecisiveness, if not diffidence; matters cease to have a narrow focus, and choices are no longer presented in black and white terms. The writing task is complex, potentially chaotic and overwhelming on first inspection. Confusion reigns, but concern about doing the right thing, by bringing matters under control, is foremost in the mind of the professional person.

For the inexperienced and unwise, the tempting practice of 'diving in', or indeed blindly following a template structure to see what develops, is an unpredictable way to attempt control of a performance-driven task. Breaking through the maelstrom is a daunting challenge and it is foolhardy to attempt to do so unaided by a distinct performance aim.

Successful performance in the writing task is where a message is unquestionably the best influential advice. It requires that customer-reader satisfaction is foremost in the mind of the writer. Customer-readers expect the writer to allow them to see the content of the message without undue effort or difficulty; the writer expects readers to further see its substance without undue uncertainty about the truth of the matter.

A successfully written product satisfies those expectations, making the truth of the matter stand. It is believable and can be trusted to shape the outcome of the work in question. The performance aim of the writer, therefore, is to reach the goal destination of the writing purpose in the condition: *that readers trust the message in the written product, readily grasping it without reservations or doubt.* Fulfilment of this aim is the desired outcome of writing as well as possible; it means averting potential common faults (intellectual and mood) with fluent, positive and purposeful communication.

It is through fluency that the writer does not let content become difficult (efficient fluency) and substance becomes obscured (effective fluency). The writer fortifies that fluency by imparting a positive outlook to communicate and a purposeful intent to reach the goal destination, that is, a 'positive purposefulness'. The whole amounts to a predictably reliable written product that readers are able to trust. When so trusted, the written product delivers influential best advice, the probability of the truth of the matter showing through to readers convincingly.

It is apposite, therefore, for the writer routinely to ask of their choice and arrangement of words:

1. How fluent am I? Are readers able to adhere to the intended meaning of the text? Are they able to get to grips with its substance?

2. How positively purposeful am I? Are readers irresistibly drawn to meaning and substance?

By querying those things, the writer makes checks and balances in the writing task. Fluency and positive purposefulness are performance yardsticks or indicators of sorts in that respect.

Performance indicators are there usually to give a measure of the success of a particular activity against the achievement of a goal, in this instance the goal-purpose *to convey best advice with influence.* In that capacity, they should be capable of frequent measurement. The performance indicator questions (above) are not capable of measurement per se, but armed with the techniques that follow in Chapter Seven, they do have a good measure of practicality. Practicality means that they will lead to corrective action.

In any case, when performance indicators are precise, measurable benchmarks and particularly deterministic of outcomes, they can be counterproductive if there is a 'dark side' of unintended consequences (Chapter Five ~ see *Unintended Consequences*).

A troubling example concerns timeliness in the accident and emergency departments of hospitals when the chosen performance indicator measured the time between patient registration and doctor attention. The nursing staff responded by encouraging paramedics to keep patients in ambulances, so delaying registration until a doctor became available. Ambulance congestion, delay and shortage resulted.

As the performance indicator questions are more qualitative than quantitative they are unlikely to have a dark side. They will serve the writer well for guiding corrective action when potential intellectual and mood faults threaten the performance of the writing task.

Successful Performance: Method

As most will know, a goal usually has a number of different ways to it, from incremental stealth to systematic proceedings. The performance aim is about carrying readers by means of believability and trust, but the pitfalls and minefield of the writing journey tend to get in the way, thwarting any semblance of control. The professional person takes control of the writing task with freely accepted responsibility for dealing with the very many instrumental factors of awareness so involved (Chapters Four and Five ~ see *Tranches* 1 and 2). Having responsibility is one thing, knowing how to apply it in a structured way to gain control of the writing task is another.

A method of approach allows the writer to stand back from the minutiae. It gives an overview and representation, providing simplification, focus and imagery to the complexity of it, from which, as far as possible, the structured way of a method of approach emerges. How to apply responsibility, between the start and finish of the writing journey, becomes clearer, with indecisiveness and diffidence no longer overwhelming the writer.

A method of approach aids active concentration. Particularly when in the form of a model, there is the direction given to the writing task through a discipline that offers predictable performance from one writing task to another. In addition, troubled motivation is helped, for the writer becomes encouraged or somewhat compelled to move forward within stages and onto the next.

The structured way to the goal destination of the writing task is a method of approach informed by the performance aim. In summary, this requires effective fluency with purposeful intent to establish trust of substance and efficient fluency with a positive outlook to establish a ready grasp of content.

The metaphor of 'a writing journey' in *Professionalism on the Page* provides the basis for an approach in the form of a conceptual model. The route of the journey is swift and safe, a highway over which the writing task progresses fluently with positive, purposeful intent, with a limited tolerance of detours.

The trust of substance through effective fluency and purposeful intent requires careful execution of any irresistible departures from the highway route. The writer tolerates detours **proportionately** only, according to the relevance and importance of the matters raised. The writer seeks always to 'stay on track'. Additionally, staying on track means that proportionate supporting material is in place to give justification for the route followed and the destination of well-founded conclusive results.

The ready grasp of content through efficient fluency with positive outlook requires carrying the reader-passengers along the highway **vicariously**, by writing as if on their behalf in tune with their situation, acknowledging their interests and concerns in one way or another. Those reader-passengers will include the writer's peers who will be looking for a journey exhibiting customary literary skill.

At all times, the attention is upon smoothly moving forward from what has already been set down or passed along the highway. The writer repeats many 'thinking steps' to examine the ground differently with each pass, looking back as much as forward **iteratively**. Working iteratively is vital to experimentation, not least to critical thinking and getting at root causes, for charting and adjusting the way ahead.

Travelling the writing journey, the writer sees the whole readership as customer-passengers with expectations to be fulfilled (vicariously). There is great pressure to embrace all things, but the writer manages that pressure and stays in control so not to allow others to push and pull the route of the writing task inappropriately (**p**roportionately). The writer keeps control by not losing sight of the goal-purpose and performance aim, looping back around when the line of argument, reasoning or expression signals unproductive outcomes. Routinely, the writer examines all matters afresh (**i**teratively).

The highway journey concept shows the association between operative modes of performance (**VIP**) in carrying out the writing task deferentially. The acronym usefully gives emphasis to the significance of the venture for the writer and reader both.

Readers will not fully trust the message in the written product unless there is an amalgamation of literary skill with subject ability. For this, those operative modes must act in combination with another of a different complexion. A procedurally substantive mode safeguards content and gives constructive onward movement through the writing task. This applies routinely and methodically in four stages as follows, for as many times as there are issues or as the work subject demands:

1) Compiling relevant documentation of the baseline situation is the first procedural stage. For example, in town planning, how else can a conclusion be reached that a proposed development would or would not be harmful to the character and appearance of an area if that very baseline condition has not been defined in a way that enables the comparison between the existing and proposed? This first procedural stage is subject **features**, which the writer must assess and define strictly according to the issues or matters under examination.

2) With the assessment and definition of subject features to hand, the writer moves to the second procedural stage concerning how the baseline situation may change in response to whatever the issues or matters bring to

it; the writer investigates *in the detail of relevant features* the unbridled **effects** of what may occur. In the town planning example, these could be an alteration in the historic character and appearance of an area by virtue of proposed contemporary design to a commercially vibrant land use.

3) After the writer establishes the effects of the issues or matters under examination, an **analysis** of those effects establishes their suitability or acceptability, the third procedural stage. In town planning, this is when public policy and standards derived therefrom come into the examination. In the example, beneficial changes by way of contrasting design and injection of activity to a run-down historic core may well be welcomed and encouraged in policy.

4) Finally, the fourth and last procedural stage is the arriving at **results** informed by component conclusions, stringently in the terms of what has gone before, particularly with reference to the start or causality of the work in question and the subsequent reasoning. The writer establishes a fusion between the end and the beginning.

The procedurally substantive performance mode completing the VIP model is **fearsome**. The **FEAR** acronym constantly reminds the writer about the dread of misadventure, especially the challenge to address mood and motivation by way of positively releasing intellectual effort, through the purposeful draw of prescribed stages, free of undue complexity. The various fears incumbent upon professional life, notably the fears of failure, of difficult people and of the unexpected, are never far away.

The complete conceptual model is the **VIP** highway of **FEAR** (VIP-FEAR). In the structured pursuit of the goal destination, the writer follows the VIP highway, advancing along it by way of FEAR. It helps the writer to travel expediently in a fluent, unified way along a dependable course, with predictable reliability. The route is not that of an indulgent 'Sunday outing', but that of an imperative business journey requiring skilful attention. It is a journey in which the distractions of scenery are irrelevant and the intent of advancing upon a destination in the desired form of the performance aim foremost.

The VIP-FEAR model-method of approach, like any model, offers simplification, focus and imagery to the complexity of the writing task, in a practical, performance-orientated manner. It prompts the writer into a way of both *thinking about* and *thinking along with* the interactive mechanisms that operate so that the whole structure for successful performance comes into view for attention; it exerts a discipline of thought that charts the route of the writing journey as it unfolds with the writing task.

The Model-Method and *Exact Writing*

Exact Writing involves a process of performance for fluency and positive purposefulness. With this process, the writer strives for accuracy, precision and clarity by responding to common intellectual and mood faults. A Code of Awareness, reflecting root causes to faults, enlightens that response. A Code of Responsibility aligns the response through various practices. The writer makes words count, as expressions of meaning and of thought, so to deliver a concise written product to the client and other readers, one that is accurate, precise and clear.

The writer considers the choice and arrangement of words with reference to fourteen thinking practices of responsibility, informed by thirty-nine factors of awareness. Each of the four operative modes of the model-method (*vicariously, iteratively, proportionately, fearsomely*) induces those practices in some way or other. How well the model-method does this, bringing all practices to the fore of the writer's mind, is a measure of its significance to *Exact Writing*.

That which follows is an appraisal of how each operative mode of performance induces the thinking practices of responsibility. The appraisal singles out what are arguably the most noticeable intents. For simplicity, the appraisal leaves aside the many intents of a more subtle nature. The appraisal adheres to the order of the acronym that states the model-method.

Firstly, thinking *vicariously* triggers these intents to responsible practices:

- unfolding the message – portraying substance graphically in line with what readers will follow to absorb.
- rationalising meaning – using the weight words

carry to readers.

- envisaging text – choosing and arranging words for the 'eye-voice' of readers.
- streamlining content – seeing through a reader 'need to know' focus.
- upholding bare results – levelling a decisive uncomplicatedness that counts for a lot in readers' eyes.
- showcasing stature – seeing through readers' eyes, looking for a customarily distinctive written product.
- manifesting facts – acting as a reader looking on in scrutiny, to be satisfied that the reporting of material facts throughout is true to their original meaning, especially when interpreting diverse 'soft' information so not to cause gratuitous controversy or offence.
- championing positive results – gauging how the written product is to serve readers in the subject work area, so to be as forceful as possible, one way or another, about it.

Secondly, thinking *iteratively* triggers these intents to responsible practices:

- unfolding the message – establishing a 'story' by pausing as it unfolds to re-evaluate and retrospectively fit and refit the component parts, for a unified whole devoid of peripheral or divergent content.
- rationalising meaning – revisiting related words and

expressions continually for potential amendment before setting down others with certitude.

- testing knowledge – making repeated backward qualifications or corrections to the source material together with subordinate amendments.
- advancing the case – looking back to go forward, taking in other lines of argument and/or bridging assumptions in order to summon sufficient supporting material.
- moderating context – undertaking backward checks by reviewing the starting position progressively to where it has led, applying necessary adjustments throughout, to avert a lost finish or an unsatisfactory closing to the written product.
- tackling impediments – taking steps backwards to see the bigger picture, for repeated attempts by other means to get past hold-ups in problem areas.
- discovering substance – going forward experimentally in an open-minded, trial and error way for expansion and fitting coverage of the subject working dealing.

Thirdly, thinking *proportionately* triggers these intents to responsible practices:

- unfolding the message – rejecting immaterial content to keep focused upon substantive and determinative matters only.
- envisaging text – keeping to knowledge-appropriate language and meaningful words and expressions,

strictly in line with the substance they are to reflect.

- streamlining content – refraining from unnecessarily sharing personal knowledge or other additional material, to exclude insignificant but overwhelming text.
- upholding bare results – resisting a 'smokescreen' of fortification in favour of straightforward, uncomplicated coverage of what has come about.
- testing knowledge – establishing the weight that source material should carry, especially where it is abundant or contradictory.
- moderating context – abandoning lines of argument that do not relate to or recover the starting position.
- activating potency – applying all of what must lie behind well-founded conclusions and results.
- championing positive results – ceasing to hold all matters in equal measure, looking always to apportion weight to the most determinative ones, to forcefully deal with what counts most.

Finally, thinking *fearsomely* triggers these intents to responsible practices:

- unfolding the message – applying structure and logic.
- showcasing stature – allowing subject proficiency to show through in literary skill.
- manifesting facts – recognising the importance of source information to all that progressively follows.
- testing knowledge – looking for a sure foundation

upon which to build subsequent analyses.

- advancing the case – finding that disconnection in subject analysis cannot be sustained and requiring commensurate accommodating analysis.
- moderating context – connecting ends to beginnings through a methodical course.
- tackling impediments – confronting difficulties with support from the uncontested demands of the recognised procedure.
- discovering substance – stretching beyond self-imposed boundaries, by sticking to imposed, procedural demands.
- activating potency – responding to the lure of straightforward sequential steps through the subject matter.

Behind this appraisal are the many instrumental factors of awareness that underlie faults and give rise to the responsible practices. These are referred to in the Code of Responsibility (Chapters Four and Five). The writer will soon realise that, when acting upon the above intents, certain instrumental factors become pivotal. For example, reader *recollection* becomes a pivotal awareness factor to the messy writer when it comes to the fault of disorder (muddled) and the responsible practice of unfolding the message. Similarly, *practical intelligence* becomes a pivotal awareness factor to the guarded writer when it comes to the fault of escalation (blurred) and the responsible practice of frankly upholding bare results.

Table 6 presents a summary of the appraisal, the

action of the model-method, by listing the responsible practices under the performance modes. The headline to each practice is the fault to which it relates, followed by the look of it. The Table gives a broad view of how the VIP-FEAR model-method of approach embraces the mechanisms of the writing task, bringing to the fore awareness and responsibility unpretentiously.

The appraisal shows that every performance mode bears down upon every performance indicator. The vicarious mode exerts most strongly upon *efficient fluency*; the iteratively and proportionately modes between them exert across the board, notably each including *positive purposefulness*; and the fearsome mode exerts most strongly upon *effective fluency*. In addition, at least half of the performance modes bring every responsible practice into play. In other words, the VIP-FEAR model-method brings all practices prominently and firmly into the mind of the writer for action.

The model-method strongly places the writer to be fluent, positive and purposeful. This is where the freely accepted responsibility of the professional person must lead, the practices for which are set out in the Code of Responsibility (Chapters Four and Five ~ *see Tranches 1 & 2*). The model-method of approach causes the Code of Responsibility and by association its counterpart that enlightens it, the Code of Awareness, to be the bedrock of *Exact Writing*. With this method of approach, the writer may confidently seek to take control of the writing task.

The Locus of *Exact Writing*

Table 6 summarises how the model-method impinges upon intellectual and mood faults through calling upon responsible practices, showing particularly the connections to performance. The whole sphere of relationships shown in the table is the place where *Exact Writing* happens; it is the locus for the action of the workings of the VIP-FEAR model.

Table 6: Action of the Model-Method

Vicariously – Iteratively – Proportionately – Fearsomely

Faults & Responsible Practices	Vicariously	Iteratively	Proportionately	Fearsomely
Efficient fluency				
disorder (muddled) unfolding	0	0	0	0
discord (vague) rationalising	0	0		
ostentation (elaborate) envisaging	0		0	
voracity (overloaded) streamlining	0		0	
escalation (blurred) upholding	0		0	
Effective Fluency				
laxity (inferior) showcasing	0			0
distortion (misleading) manifesting	0			0
incongruity (unsound) testing		0	0	0
incoherence (fragile) advancing		0		0
misconstruction (unstable) moderating		0	0	0
Positive Purposefulness				
partiality (uneven) tackling		0		0
fixation (seductive) discovering		0		0
distraction (impenetrable) activating			0	0
prevarication (poised) championing	0		0	

Performance – Proficiency

The impetus of the codes of awareness and of responsibility is for fluent performance with a positive outlook and purposeful intent. The codes demonstrate the complex process of performance that is the writing task. It is a process aimed at trust, for customer-reader satisfaction. The writer seeks to accomplish that trust with a fitting choice and arrangement of words. Given the complexity of the writing task process, a structured approach to inform that choice is crucial. Such an approach uses the metaphor of the writing journey in a conceptual model, which is the hub to *Exact Writing*. The VIP highway of FEAR model orientates the professional person to control the writing task with accuracy, precision and clarity, for an impressive, trustworthy written product.

Insight

Subject expertise, including professional attributes, is insufficient alone to inform the writing task. Well beyond that is an intellectual effort that serves the demands of the writing task itself. It goes broadly outside typical academic style documentation, which follows well-established, narrow lines of a linear, logical progression from the general to the specific. The accomplished professional approaches the writing task with a wide-ranging, resourceful 'thinking discipline' for the eclectic process of performance. See it as a 'backwardly-forward' operational process. Like chess, only ever take a step forward after establishing that it is secure to do so and/or will bring the best positional advantage. The accomplished professional, continually with each impending placing of word and phrase, looks all around to feel the presence of readers and then back to see the course of reasoning, proceeding always to cement or regain a fluency and positive purposefulness that readers will greatly value and admire.

Exact Writing ~ The Discipline

Thinking the writing process through

Fulfil the goal destination of the writing purpose with the aim of doing it as well as possible. Advance the writing task as a process of performance along the particular route of the writing journey unravelled by a conceptual model, VIP-FEAR. Think operationally with due deference to content and substance in these terms:

- vicariously – put readers centrally in mind as present and looking critically on.
- iteratively – sense to look back when writing forward on the page, keeping sight of the writing purpose, especially the start and finish ends of the

writing journey.

- proportionately – focus unrelentingly on the way ahead, entertaining minor departures only, allowing others exceptionally but not beyond their worth, so that readers understand that all is heading for the same destination.
- fearsomely – see the requirements of the subject matter in a simple, methodical way that serves as writing stages (features, effects, analysis, results) for ensuring substantive content, particularly through the pre-empting of reluctance and risk aversion from fears.

Mentally chart the route of the writing journey to drive fluently and steer with positive purposefulness towards the goal destination with surety.

Chapter Seven
THE HAND OF
FLUENCY

If people knew how hard I work to gain my mastery,
it would not seem so wonderful at all.

Michelangelo 1475-1564
Italian painter & sculptor

Concerns

Successful performance is a wonderfully masterful thing. Professionals need to apply hard work to accomplish it. Sadly, too many do not understand that connection and give way to interest in how little of it will suffice. Techniques make the connection to harness work effort into its proper place and allow talent full expression.

> What hard work is called for in the writing task? How is the writer to engage in it, to choose and arrange words judiciously?

This chapter sets out a number of techniques that help the writer to perform masterfully with the model-method of approach. The use of the bold font gives emphasis to the first mentioning of these.

Particular techniques assist the driver in mastering a successful journey along the charted route, across challenging terrain and territory.

Accomplishment through Effort

There is no place for the slovenly writer in the professional world. The unaccomplished writer may adhere to strict rules and produce grammatically correct work, but such work will be prone to many faults when it comes to loose expression from poor thinking. Accomplishment is built upon awareness and responsibility, which open up the way for great care through orchestrated effort. In the end, the effort will pay dividends in several ways, not least when the writer avoids reworking faulty prose.

To recap, *Exact Writing* treats the writing task as a complex process of performance focussed towards a performance aim. A method of approach, in the form of a thinking discipline, brings orientation and organisation to it, allowing performance indicators concerning *fluency* and *positive purposefulness* to guide the writer towards accomplishment.

Fluency unites the subject matter of the written product with readers in two ways. Efficient fluency connects content so that readers comfortably understand the meaning, whereas effective fluency projects substance so that readers perceive the essence of the writer's argument or view. With a positive outlook to communicate and a purposeful intent to reach the desired outcome, the writer appeals to readers, presenting them with a predictably reliable written product, which is both convincing and influential (Chapter Six ~ see *Goals, Meaning and Purpose* and *Successful Performance: The Aim*).

The writer applies techniques to orchestrate the thinking discipline of the model-method of approach into effort or hard work; they are the bedrock of expertise, that is, of expert skill, knowledge or judgement. The techniques that follow are fundamental in marshalling and directing mental effort in particular ways; they are 'headline' techniques that convert thought into action. Each has a crucial role in aiding the responsible practices towards averting intellectual or mood faults, for successful writing performance.

The writer applies the techniques as masterfully as possible. Alongside customary literary skill, the writer's style shows through, revealing personality and voice, as well as attitude to readership (Chapter One ~ see *Seeing, Speaking and Hearing* and *Inherent Significance*, also Chapter Three ~ see *Communication Requirements*).

Efficient Fluency: Connecting Content

Faced with an inefficient text, readers will have doubts about the written product, having uncertainties about its content. Readers will not forgive the writer who makes them struggle to understand the meaning.

Words, phrases and sentences form instant images in the minds of readers and trigger interpretation of meaning. Readers will readily grasp meaning with confidence when there are strong word images. The writer must write very much with the 'eye-voice' of readers firmly in mind (Chapter One ~ see *Speaking, Seeing and Hearing*). A poor choice, handling and arrangement of words will result in weak images and readers will not recognise where they are.

In fictional writing, the author pictures the scene and shows it evocatively through words, often in preference to merely telling it. Here is a borrowed example from Nigel Watts, from his book *Write a Novel and Get it Published*, with which his students of creative writing see the weakness of merely 'telling' and the strength of 'showing':

- 'It was a dark and stormy night. He walked slowly to the window and watched the devastation caused by the wind' (telling).
- 'The moon was full. He shuffled to the window and watched the storm tearing at the limbs of the willow' (showing).

The former does not conjure up an image of drama and interest in the mind of the reader; the latter does and the reader will easily form the physical and emotional image intended.

Metaphors and figures of speech that turn language away from literal meaning are especially important in that regard, for they shape interpretation. Different metaphors allow us to think differently about the same thing. Therein lies the difficulty for the pragmatic writer who, in any case, resists using metaphors and figures of speech for fear of eliciting an emotional response that would potentially comprise objectivity (Chapter One ~ see *Words and Connotations*). The professional person has only the 'telling' of the message to work with in promoting images for the eye-voice of the reader.

Readers are unlikely to read every word on the page once they believe they have arrived at – potentially wrongly – a valid impression or interpretation. It is the end of a rapid, repetitive process of adjustment, one in which the eye jumps about looking for clues about the intended image of meaning: the reader searches around the word or phrase in the sentence and the sentence in the paragraph. Too many words get in the way because they misuse reading time and tire readers who are then tempted to stick with first impressions.

The probable reason why writers run the risk of wordiness is that there is an ingrained desire for sophistication and a distrust of simple expressions, originating probably from childhood when the use of difficult words and concepts earned unqualified praise. The writer demonstrates an understanding and thereby feels important. Other reasons may relate to mood faults, especially in that experience and peer pressure in professional life lead to cautious actions and the cynic will say that 'mistiness is the mother of safety' (Chapter Five ~ see *Faults of the Cobra Effect*).

The technique of **compaction** is one way of combatting wordiness of this nature, by amplifying readers' appreciation of meaning in fewer words. Strong word images are likely to show through to the reader when the writer uses compact expressions.

Everything that is exact (accurate, precise and clear) is usually capable of short expression; eminent people have stated so. The writer should know that 'simplicity is the ultimate sophistication' (Leonardo da Vinci). Also, that the objective is to 'say all that has to be said in the fewest possible words, or readers will be sure to skip them, and in the plainest possible words or readers will certainly misunderstand them' (Ruskin).

Why would the writer run the risk of wordiness with, for example, circumlocution (roundabout expression) and passive verbs (more about these later) when a far more compact expression is possible. Take this example:

In the meantime, it is considered necessary that there be a meeting of case officers for the northern district to discuss the need to protect the conservation area more consistently in these present circumstances. (34 words)

Meanwhile, case officers for the northern district must meet to discuss whether they need to act immediately to give consistent protection to the conservation area. (25 words)

Wordiness occurs when sentences are too diffuse, especially where closely related parts of sentences stand separate from one another. This demands too much of the reader's memory, for subject or topic 'ends' are far removed from 'beginnings'. Here is an example of that:

Under current planning policy, if any development is proposed outside the built-up boundary or on back-land in residential areas where the density exceeds 30 dwellings per hectare and where there is no available brownfield

> *land within 5 kilometres, then* <u>*planning permission will be*</u> <u>*refused.*</u> (44 words)

When the writer unites the topic end with the beginning, the message is more compact with a stronger image, thus:

> <u>*Under current planning policy, planning permission will*</u> <u>*be refused*</u> *for any development proposed outside the built-up area, or on back-land in areas exceeding 30 dwellings per hectare with available brownfield land within 5 kilometres.* (34 words)

Excessive phrases make matters worse. They comprise wasted words and are commonplace. There are very many examples in everyday use, such as:

In the event that	*if*
Along the lines of	*like*
Notwithstanding the fact that	*although*
If the circumstances should arise that	*when*
In the light of the fact that	*as*

Readers may wonder what they must grasp in addition to what the writer could have conveyed more compactly.

Wordiness occurs also through redundant terms. These include tautologies and other repetition, empty modifiers (such as *to all intents and purposes*) and abstract nouns (such as *it is a fact that*). Negative constructions (*it is not unlikely that*), metadiscourse (writing about your writing thus: *the purpose of this note is...*) and circumlocution (*as in the earlier example above*).

Another technique with which to help the eye-voice of readers is **thread**.

There should be no surprises or confusion for readers

in what words the writer chooses to set down. The technique of laying down a thread enables readers to see with an unblemished focus the emergent meaning as intended; it telegraphs the way ahead. Here, the writer connects sentences and paragraphs one to another with a unifying thought, which is the thread. The fictional writer will plait several threads. The absence of a thread leaves readers unprepared for what developing or emerging thought the writer has. A thread allows readers instantly to retrace steps to follow the intended meaning comfortably and never to feel lost or abandoned by the writer.

It is with a subtle skill that the writer lays down a thread. The topic sentences and signpost words of the standard academic pattern of writing provide readers with clues about paragraph content. They are unlikely, however, to give clues as to the meaning of words and phrases where they loosely or brokenly connect, especially from one paragraph to the next. The placing of thread sentences, often at the end of paragraphs to link one to another, helps the writer to sustain a thread image so that words unfold to the reader for secure interpretation.

A unifying thread cannot exist when words unfold inconsistently. This is where there are internal inconsistencies or lack of cohesion in the choice or arrangement of words from one part of the text to another or wherever vagueness creeps in. Professional people are prone to sustain poor composition with the practice of substituting overworked words with others. Some may perceive the need to disguise repetition. For example, why replace 'substantial' with 'considerable' when subsequently referring to something of equal substance? In any event, are those things not, in fact, significant, but in different ways, and is there not a better way of saying it? After all, what are readers to make of it? Is the writer saying something different or not? If two words are genuinely suitable, adopt a convention and stick to it!

The techniques of compaction and thread direct the writer's effort towards accurate, precise and clear, thoughtful expression. In the example above, what is the real meaning of the matter: is it 'substantial' or 'considerable' or 'significant'? (What is most accurate?) If the latter, what is it significant to and how? Alternatively, is it a combination of these things, and in which case, which one counts the most? Why continue to write forward on a broad front through interchanging words when readers require a narrowing focus for a recognisable thread? (Where is the precision?) Why make it hard for readers to know what to rely upon for interpreting the intended meaning? (What clarity is left?)

All words do have different meanings, but some meanings do intersect, with shades of meaning often confusingly close. Synonyms are not always words with much the same meaning, and any subtlety in meaning offers fine-tuning of expression – never should the writer ignore or abuse that fact. For example, it happens that a successful complaint, if not a legal action, to a Planning Inspectorate's decision letter (statement of reasoning) can derive from the misuse of just one word or from its contribution to the poor precision and accuracy of just one sentence. With English, there is ample scope for accurate, precise and clear, thoughtful expression, whereby the thought voice of the writer successfully converts to the eye-voice of the reader, to make a connection with strong contextual images from compact, threaded text.

Unfortunately, a connection tainted by the writer's preference for complication or sophistication, a complexity over simplicity, takes invidious hold of the writing task at the outset. After then, the writer makes some effort to remedy it, but it becomes a time casualty. 'If I had more time I would have written less' aptly conveys the fact that, for many, the achievement of simplicity is not built into the writing task but is taken as a luxury addition. The technique of **lucidity** directs the writer's efforts to discard inappropriate words and phrases on the basis that they do not yield instantly recognisable true meanings.

Lucidity defines the quality of the language the writer uses. Words and their arrangement have lucidity when their true meaning is before the eyes of readers completely and absolutely, without recourse to other understanding gleaned from elsewhere in the text, or beyond. Heavyweight words in lightweight applications are examples of poor lucidity because meaning becomes deadened and thereby obscure. Also, there is no word left when you need it. Distinction expands our scope for expression and its removal constrains it.

From the example above, is 'considerable' not a heavyweight word in comparison to 'substantial', and that in turn in comparison to 'significant'? With big words in little contexts and many other misconstructions, the true meaning is absent and readers have to search to retrieve it somehow. Applying the technique of lucidity, the writer makes words carry their own weight and work with immediacy to serve the eye-voice of readers. As George Orwell once said, 'let the meaning choose the word'.

In the final analysis, professional people communicate for a living and cannot afford to alienate any reader by discourteously burdening them with the task of translating embedded obscure meaning. Writing with the propriety of lucidity is an indispensable skill and the greatest affront to it is the impolite language of professional jargon.

Professional jargon is a private language of some technical precision, from one member to another, and it is entirely justifiable when it does not subvert comprehension of the intended meaning. However, jargon laden private exchanges have limited use because there is always a risk that content from these will slip into a wider readership where readers, if not swayed, will become puzzled and annoyed.

Jargon is not just a precise technical language. Non-technical jargon, especially, is difficult to spot when it pervades the working environment. A recent example comes from a family court hearing when a judge berated a social services officer for the jargon-laden written report submitted because there was a risk that the other parties present would fail to understand it fully, if at all. One of many phrases singled out by the judge was: 'Due to SH's apparent difficulties identifying the concerns, I asked her to convey a narrative about her observations'. The judge asked, 'What would be wrong in saying 'I asked her to tell me'?' To 'convey a narrative' has no immediacy of true meaning, but to 'tell' has; there is greater lucidity to it, being simply obvious.

The vocabulary of the professional person must contain only words that are acceptable by general consent. Some jargon words and phrases have long established themselves that way, such as 'green belt' and 'infrastructure'. Others, new or popular, must not prematurely extend that vocabulary without such consent, however deserving.

Readers will become confused or burdened with searching elsewhere for meaning when the writer fails to set down the right word or expression. They will skip words or misunderstand the intended meaning unless the writer's expertise connects content through compaction, thread and lucidity (Chapter Three ~ see especially *Reading Habits* and *Reading Capacity*).

Effective Fluency: Projecting Substance

Faced with an ineffective text, readers will have reservations about the written product, being unsure of its substance. Readers will feel dissatisfied if left irresolute by the writer. Not only do readers need to be able to understand what the writer intended, but also crucially they need to be able to take in the information or substance presented (Chapter Three ~ see especially *Communication Requirements*).

In the world of advertising and social marketing, vividly presented information receives attention because it stands out and is easy to recall. In the workplace, the substance of the written product must similarly stand out if it is to receive due attention. Through compaction, thread and lucidity the writer shows readers the content of where they are in the written product, but not its substance. The substance before them does not stand out for attention unless it plainly has consequences relating to what is to come.

Fictional writing has a plot. A plot is the cause-and-effect sequence of events in a story. It highlights the important points that have important consequences and does not include memorable scenes where they do not relate to other events. There are characters, unfolding issues and conflict, and these interrelate in a particular way to move the action forward, making the plot.

In pragmatic writing, there is no plot. The writer moves the action forward in the written product, the cause and effect interrelationships, by way of the technique of shaping a **thesis**. The *Oxford English Dictionary* tells us that a thesis is 'a proposition to be maintained or proved'. Unlike a thread, which may vary throughout and is willowy, the thesis is the solid backbone to the written product. Without a clearly defined thesis, readers will begin to doubt whether the writer has correctly addressed the work in question and, in any case, whether the content adequately supports the conclusions and results. Applying the technique of shaping a thesis is about giving a fitting structure to the written product.

A fitting structure lets readers see where they are going in the process of recognising, assimilating and integrating the substance immediately before them. It aids reader retention and recall, which are indispensable to the critical or close reading that most readers will expect to be able to do at some point or other for them to establish substance (Chapter Three ~ see *Reading Habits*). Furthermore, it brings satisfying closure to the work in question by connecting the end of the written product to its beginning. The important point being that an ending to a story is always implicit in its beginning and readers would not read it if its end is missing.

The structure of many written products adheres to some format or other. Often this is a house style or a fail-safe device to rein in otherwise errant writers, forcing and limiting their attention to particular matters. There is a tendency for a format to become a 'comfort blanket' that negates the thinking discipline to the performance process that is the writing task. The thesis therein is poorly shaped and substance does not stand out.

A structure that unmistakably connects the finish with the start of the written product projects the substance of all content in-between when it forms the solid backbone of the thesis. The technique of **directness** marshals the writer's efforts to make that backbone as solid as possible. Applying the technique of directness, the writer gets straight to the point as quickly as possible.

A writer who gets to the point as quickly as possible has the best chance of projecting substance to readers. This is due to the principle of least effort, or path of least resistance, which is a truth commonly experienced when it comes to such things as journeying between two places, especially on foot. According to this principle, the information-seeking behaviour of readers will direct their effort to the most convenient means of searching in the least exacting way available. Readers stop searching as soon as they find minimally acceptable results.

With the technique of directness, therefore, the writer manages the willowy threads to the subject matter, pulling these as taut as possible and pruning relentlessly for readers to take the substance of it within their grip. The skill is for the writer to know what to leave out, and skilful writers aim to leave out as much relevant content as they dare, not rehearsing matters unnecessarily. The writer directly addresses materially determinative content only and even then excludes much that can be 'taken as read'. The writer's aim is always to write less than is possible so that words and their arrangement have more impact: 'less is more', as they say and everyday examples of this abound.

Managing threads through directness is particularly challenging, especially as these are likely to comprise a loose mixture of data and wide-ranging information. In any event, when searching through content for substance readers will wish to see the writer treating matters fairly, without personal influence or bias. The substance must not only stand out to readers, but also cross their threshold for minimally acceptable results. Writing with customary literary skill is a prerequisite for crossing that threshold. Communicating objective analysis through honest, dispassionate impartiality is the key.

It is with the technique of **register** that the writer can demonstrate those qualities. Many professional people think they know how to use an appropriate register, but in truth give insufficient attention to it. With limited understanding, they slavishly adopt what is presented to them as a 'professional writing style'. A return to basics from a different perspective helps to show the necessity of a much more intelligent use of register for effective fluency; the value of an appropriate register cannot be overstressed.

The register is the gauge of how impersonal the text is. Within the bounds of correct English usage, there is a choice between three varieties of register, as follows:

Informal/personal	semi-formal	formal/impersonal
you can try to	one might try to	an attempt may be made to
don't bother me	you need not	it is unnecessary to

The informal register has a conversational tone, whereas, in the formal register, direct speech and colloquial expressions (e.g. 'beat about the bush') are absent and impersonal language is used. This requires the avoidance of personal pronouns (i.e. I, me, you etc.) and, notably in England, there is a customary adherence to a passive voice (e.g. 'an attempt may' in place of 'you can'). The person 'doing' the verb is absent, or present *after* instead of *before* the verb in phrases of passive construction.

Applying a formal register that disengages the writer from the action, to give a detachment, is to write in the 'third person' (he/she/the reader etc.). Where objectivity is critical, such as in scientific English, writers are motivated to use the passive construction as the chief means of expressing an impersonal, knowledgeable point of view as an expert authority. Even so, it has its drawbacks and is not without criticism.

In some instances, the formal register can mislead the reader, intentionally or otherwise, through missing information (the personal and active pieces). This makes it popular in political circles because of the potential for deliberate ambiguity, which provides the option of deniability. Where passive verbs predominate, the text inclines towards dull, bland and convoluted constructions that overwhelm readers who do not see substance standing out boldly.

Through university training, experience or peer expectation, professional people often have no more than drifted, consciously or not, into the use of the formal register of the academic world. The focus there is squarely on truth-telling accuracy with the pursuit of subjects in all directions at a leisurely pace in a discursive, exploratory, reflective and hypothetical manner. Convoluted expressions inevitably result, notably from the use of the passive voice, which is in the interests of establishing objectivity.

The professional person, however, is not scholarly and does not live in that academic world, but is experienced through everyday practice. Judgement contributes substantially to the expertise of the jobbing professional person (Chapter Two ~ see *Judgement*). The professional person is different also due to the work areas involved that mainly concern the exercise of executive authority outright, or by delegation: by the client, the board or the committee, or a superior. If not executive authority, then the work areas are often performed in some form of official capacity for stipulated outcomes.

Written work that serves such dealings does not push against or define boundaries of knowledge or understanding through research and learning. Consequently, the written work of professional people is less proof-laden and there is little need of backing it up with extensive citations, which are imperative in academic literature. Much of the so-called evidence in written products underpins the expert opinion sought and is shades of grey, reflecting the subjectivity of the professional field in question and the contribution of professional experience. Academic evidence, on the other hand, is more likely to be theoretically or scientifically correct or incorrect: black or white. Readers will not expect the professional person to produce heavily laden theoretical text.

What readers expect comes from their presuppositions about the written product. It is impossible for them to think about the text other than in ways people may have led them to expect. The formal register remains the expected 'code of good manners' because it is the variety that is furthest removed from speech and the limitations of a conversational tone (Chapter One ~ see *Transmitted Words*). The impersonal and passive forms of the formal register translate in the minds of readers to objectivity, courtesy, authority and legitimacy, attributes that carry influence (Chapter Two ~ see *Literary Skill*, notably 'weapons of influence'). The writer must be ever-mindful that the tone of the 'telling of it' determines the interpretation.

For those reasons, the professional person would be unwise not to use the formal register. The wise professional person projects to readers the objective, dispassionate impartiality they rightfully expect, but does so by liberating the formal register from its academic origins in the interests of making substance stand out effectively. The writer gives particular attention to active verb constructions for livelier sentences that overcome dull, bland and convoluted constructions.

A formal register is not necessarily rooted in passive verb constructions, and the skill is not to forsake active verb constructions prematurely. For example, take this passive verb construction and its replacement with an active verb construction:

- *Steps will have to <u>be taken</u> to ascertain the applicant's ownership.*
- *The Council will <u>trace</u> what the applicant owns.*

With the passive verb construction, the message looks tentative because the writer leaves open the question of who should act, whether the writer, the receiver or the applicant. In the active verb construction, the writer uses fewer words to convey the message positively and directly, without uncertainty as to who must act. This is never an automatic 'rule-of-thumb' affair, however, because the passive form will not always be less concise, positive or direct, and may carry the advantage of looking more authoritative. Unquestionably, an intelligent use of the register is of paramount importance.

Readers will become unsettled and troubled by having to unearth what substance there is in the written product unless the writer's expertise provides a fitting structure through thesis, directness and register. A fitting structure usually abets reading habits, especially that of the speed-reader, and it helps reading capacity in terms of note-taking etc. (Chapter Three ~ see *Reading Habits* and *Reading Capacity*). The structure image of the text itself is a first rapid means of communication that will aid perception of substance if done well.

Positive Purposefulness: Imparting Appeal

Faced with an unappealing, lifeless text, readers will be uninspired by the written product, being struck by a poor image of the writer's appetite for the content and substance. Readers will be disinclined to value a mood-impaired writer's reluctant offering. The writer must communicate commitment, drive and enthusiasm infectiously.

Some recent studies of social media, namely Facebook and Twitter, indicate that a type of 'emotional contagion', a convergence, occurs with written messages between a sender and the receiver. The mood of the writer is very much inclined to transfer to the reader despite the absence of non-verbal cues. This may well be due to the conversational nature of the exchange, which is in contrast to the formal register of the professional person.

Even so, with written products, prose lays bare the intellect of the professional person (Chapter One ~ see *Inherent Significance*). Additionally, readers look for signs within the written product of the stature of the professional person, to be struck by the legitimacy it carries (Chapter Two ~ see *Literary Skill*). Stature includes the personality traits of conscientiousness, emotional intelligence and resilience (Chapter Two ~ see *Personality*). The condition of these attributes will invariably show through to readers in written work.

Research demonstrates that the emotions displayed by employees directly influence the emotional state of the customer. Some in the professional workplace may well attempt to write with intentional emotional contagion, considering themselves 'employees' and readers 'customers', as with the business representation earlier (Chapter Six ~ see *The Goal of Customer Satisfaction*). Although customers may well appreciate a positive outlook of employees towards the organisation in which they work, they will see through positive affective displays of behaviour directed at them if there is a lack of authenticity.

The professional person must act not only competently, but also with honesty and integrity (Chapter Two ~ see

Conduct). To appeal to readers through a positive outlook and purposeful intent, the professional person can write to accentuate the positives and not stray into the grey area of manipulation due to intentional emotional contagion (Chapter One ~ see *Words and Connotations*). A way of doing that is to be mindful of narrative technique.

The novelist has complete freedom of expression, where mystery and suspense are powerful components. Essentially, through many devices, the novelist is managing information for attention, often by putting questions and issues and delaying answers. Whereas the professional person has greatly circumscribed freedom of expression, not least through the register, style guides and the like, narrative technique has a place in the writing journey. After all, what these have in common is that both are writing a story for attention in active support of the conclusions or outcomes reached.

Emotions or moods transfer to readers because of the personal choices made by the writer, owing to a great many ways to arrange words within the rules of grammar (Chapter One ~ see *Speaking, Seeing and Hearing*). The writer makes personal choices in vocabulary and expression (diction and syntax) and over time develops a particular style of writing. Word choices include from abstract to concrete, general to specific. Sentence choices include the different positions that subordinate clauses may take and the density, length and weight of the whole. The style of the writer reveals both personality and voice, giving a distinctive character to the written product.

Professional people are equipped with authentic motivation and are well placed for mood resilience (Chapter Five ~ see *Responsibility – Opposing Negative Forces*). Furthermore, the professional person will have a commanding tone (Chapter One ~ see *Inherent Significance*). These impart the basis of a dynamic writing style. The technique of **thrust** allows the writer to develop that style further. It involves the timing and content of the release of information to shape a form of 'narrative thrust', underlain by the unifying thought(s) of *thread(s)* and the structural backbone of the *thesis*. Thrust is about command, urgency and momentum.

In applying the technique of thrust, the writer chooses the strongest words, avoiding the trap of 'big' words for little occasions, and arranges them in the order that gives a commanding position to what is most important. Usually, this is with sentences that put the main point in the middle or at the end, where a single subordinate clause precedes it. The writer sweeps readers dynamically along by switching between levels of detail to give pace and contrast and by foreshadowing what is to come. The writer makes topic sentences particularly powerful to serve in that connection as 'hooks' and 'anchors'.

Thrust through pace and contrast may come across to the reader in several ways, including by the abruptness and assertiveness of the 'magic of three'. This is the phenomenon whereby a series of three parallel words, phrases or clauses can add rhythm and cadence to the sound of the language. Known as a *tricolon*, each of its three parts is of the same length and structure and it is used to great effect in passionate rhetoric to inspire and persuade. An often-quoted example is: *"Tell me and I forget. Teach me and I remember. Involve me and I learn"* (Benjamin Franklin). A very simple tricolon is *the good, the bad and the ugly*, which has far more impact than merely writing *the good and the bad*.

In the dispassionate but influential register of the professional person, there is a valid place for tricolons where content or substance can be legitimately organised and expressed into threes. Take this example: *the proposed development would be unsightly due to its scale* lacks thrust when scale alone does not fully convey the impact; by adding content in the sentence, rather than separately, write the point more assertively as *the proposed development would be unsightly due to its scale, bulk and mass*, then elaborate each.

The writer communicates a positive outlook with a purposeful intent through a thrust that leaves little room for negative tendencies. These are manifest particularly in expressions that look apologetic or obtuse. Apologetic writers accentuate what they do not know, rather than what they do know; obtuse writers accentuate what they do not think, rather than what they do think. The favourite culprit amongst professionals is that of being obtuse with the use of expressions such as 'It is not thought that …', or in the active voice, 'I do not think that …'. Readers and specifically the client are not interested in what is not thought by the writer or others and rightly so; they want to know what is thought and the written word is there to communicate that (Chapter One ~ see

Inherent Significance).

Readers have an interest in the written product for many different reasons and they come to it with particular temperaments. The written product should have a certain alignment in response (Chapter Three ~ see *Readers' Interests*). Even so, readers are likely to be unreceptive of the message in the written product when it does not resonate with them. With the technique of **resonance,** the writer fully acknowledges the point of view or strength of the argument that readers have because readers will otherwise feel ignored. In any event, a contrary view almost certainly has value, which the writer does not neglect. The writer sees the good in readers and does not take an adversarial position.

The writer may build upon a contrary view by taking a wider or different perspective to tackle 'root causes' to show how the various matters sit, strengths and weaknesses all, one to another (Chapter Five ~ see *Unintended Consequences*). It is best to keep matters general and not fuel opportunity for disagreement by going into unnecessary detail. The written product is, in effect, a target for criticism and challenge for hostile readers and 'losing parties', and it is best that the writer keeps that target as small as possible. The essential point is that with the technique of resonance, the writer works with readers and not against them, positively and purposefully, to achieve a balanced view.

The techniques of thrust and resonance greatly help the writer to develop an appealing writing style in the face of unhelpful moods and poor motivation brought on by a difficult workplace environment. It is with responsible mood management, however, that the core of the negativity is addressed (Chapter Five ~ see *Mood Management and Coping Strategies*). The technique of **assimilation** helps the writer absorb and suppress unhelpful moods for movement into a better emotional state so that the writing style inclines to be naturally appealing.

The demotivating grey mood of anxiety, responsible for much of the mood faults examined earlier, sits on an emotional scale of considerable complexity. The professional person harvests the feedback that emotions give in order to turn negativity into personal insight for confronting unused potential. Such personal insight shows the value of 'doing my best to make the best of it', for it aids positive thoughts for relieving uncomfortable feelings. By reaching for the best-feeling thought available at the time and repeating the effort continually, incremental improvement and eventual movement step by step up the emotional scale occur, say from fear to discouragement, to frustration, to optimism and beyond.

The technique of assimilation is about letting the experience be the way it is and moving on upwards. It permits the writer to become less self-centred and, at the very least, abandon the negative victim/attack mode of feeling hard-done-by and thirst for some redress. Assimilation opens the way for a bearing driven by purpose, of seeing the point or importance of the work in question and the writing task in hand.

There is a distinct purpose to being professional and

particularly to having literary skill (Chapter Two). There is especially the writing purpose of conveying best advice with influence (Chapter One ~ see *Inherent Significance*). The professional person has a purpose born out of an awareness and responsibility that define what to do and how well to do it. Knowing your purpose gives focus and motivation to the task in hand; it concentrates effort and energy upon what is important and gives meaning to the workplace. Meaningless work, not overwork, is often a trigger for demotivating moods.

Studies have shown that a busy working life with a modicum of stress is beneficial to moods, motivation and health (a *tricolon!*). There is the stress associated with unsupportive colleagues and also that with the disposition of readers (Chapter Five ~ see *Mood Management and Coping Strategies* and Chapter Three ~ see *Readers' Interests*, respectively). Stress forces the professional person to make decisions and take responsibility, which has the effect of absorbing, suppressing or, indeed, lifting unhelpful moods.

The technique of assimilation, of absorbing or suppressing unhelpful moods, lets purpose prevail. Some motivational-type theorists suggest fixing the mind upon certain affirmations to lift oneself into a more beneficial state (known as the 'law of attraction'). According to this law, a positive thought attracts others and an eventual positive outcome will happen, in the belief that you create your own reality. Similarly, it explains why a downward spiral of negativity can take hold.

Negativity will threaten the standard of the written

product in some way at some time when readers will wrestle with following assuredly its message to the desired outcome (Chapter Six ~ see *Successful Performance: The Aim*). The writer's expertise gives vitality to the written product, through thrust, resonance and assimilation, imparting reader appeal.

Techniques and *Exact Writing*

The discipline of the model-method of approach aligns the thinking practices of responsibility to be at the hub of *Exact Writing* (Chapter Six ~ see *Table 6 – Action of the Model-Method*). The headline techniques, above, directly or indirectly help cement these practices into work effort and give crucial coverage overall in the writing task to successfully shape the written product. Foremost examples of this appear in the assessment below, by reference to the Code of Responsibility (Chapter Four ~ see *Code of Responsibility – Tranche 1* and Chapter Five ~ *Code of Responsibility – Tranche 2*).

- compaction gives strong word images that benefit the practices of envisaging text, seeing the arrangement of words through the reader's 'eye-voice', and streamlining content, freeing text of needless elaboration.
- thread sets down unifying thought(s) that benefit(s) the practices of rationalising meaning, averting the potential for confusion, and, unfolding the message, showing a 'story' for contextual interpretation.
- lucidity offers instantly recognisable true meanings

that benefit the practice of upholding bare results, narrowing the communication gap between writer and reader.

- thesis provides a solid backbone that benefits the practices of advancing the case, leaving no gaps in reasoning, and moderating context, keeping the start-finish ends in plain view.
- directness gets straight to the point as quickly as possible that benefits testing knowledge, organising inputs and the like by the weight they carry.
- register gives a detachment that benefits showcasing stature, setting apart the writer from everyday ability, and manifesting facts, yielding faithful influential content.
- thrust applies command, urgency and momentum that benefit championing positive results, reaching inescapable conclusions.
- resonance sees the good in readers that benefits discovering substance, returning balanced, true and best results.
- assimilation absorbs and suppresses unhelpful moods that benefit the practices of tackling impediments, searching for what lies beyond, and activating potency, aiming always to prove capable.

Shaping the Written Product

Table 7 summarises how techniques benefit responsible practices to shape the written product, for fluency and positive purposefulness.

Table 7: Techniques for Shaping the Written Product

	Efficient Fluency			Effective Fluency			Positive Purposefulness		
	Compaction	Thread	Lucidity	Thesis	Directness	Register	Thrust	Resonance	Assimilation
Responsible Practices									
unfolding		0							
rationalising		0							
envisaging	0								
streamlining	0								
upholding			0						
showcasing						0			
manifesting						0			
testing					0				
advancing				0					
moderating				0					
tackling									0
discovering								0	
activating									0
championing							0		

Performance – Expertise

With the way of *Exact Writing*, the writer follows a model-method of approach to activate a thinking discipline for many responsible practices and considers the choice and arrangement of words in that context. There are many techniques the writer may deploy for cementing such thinking into work effort to shape the organisation of the text for performance. Nine headline techniques give a comprehensive coverage. From the detailed refinement of *lucidity* to the broad adjustment of *assimilation*, work effort aligns to the performance indicators by way of three techniques impinging upon each one. The particular use of techniques defines the expertise and personal writing style of the writer. Readers see and appreciate an accomplished style that efficiently executes effective communication with commitment, drive and enthusiasm, notably: fluency with positive purposefulness.

Insight

The customary literary skill of professional people communicates the personal attributes of objectivity, authority, courtesy and legitimacy. The process of performance that is the writing task demands much more of the professional person, which is down to personal writing style. It requires an expertise developed through mastery of techniques that equip the writer to apply rigour with vigour when putting into operation the model-method of approach.

Exact Writing ~ The Work Effort

Applying effort to the writing process

Advance along the VIP highway of FEAR industriously. Carry out the writing task with work effort suitably harnessed by fundamental, headline techniques as follows:

- compaction – amplify meaning by stripping away wordiness, yielding best eye-voice images.
- thread – chart unifying thought(s), eradicating surprises or confusion.
- lucidity – show instantly recognisable true meaning, without recourse to context.
- thesis – provide a solid backbone of direction and course, from head to toe, connecting the start with its finish.
- directness – get straight to the point as quickly as possible.
- register – apply a trusted tone with impersonal yet lively expression, taking advantage of the 'weapons of influence'.
- thrust – inject an urgency with momentum from pace and contrast, showing commitment and enthusiasm.
- resonance – get in tune with readers and never let confrontation or alienation take hold
- assimilation – absorb or suppress unhelpful moods with mood management before they do any harm.

Drive responsibly with a skilful effort to navigate with the writing task the route of the writing journey successfully.

IV. HINDSIGHT

JOURNEY'S END

It is imperative to learn from experience. Even with instructive experience through coaching and mentoring, travelling the *Exact Writing* way is a trial and error process when it becomes 'hands on'. Part IV of *Professionalism on the Page* is about how to benefit from hands-on experience in performing the writing task

Having doubts, especially when other work pressures are commonplace, is the key. In any event, a 'writer's remorse' is likely to take hold, akin to 'buyer's remorse' when a recent purchase, upon reflection, ceases to look good value for money. By looking critically at work pressures and doubts about the standard of the recently completed written product, the journey's end, the writer becomes fortified for the next occasion (Chapter Eight).

Part IV is a self-debriefing of the writer-driver to see how successful the writing journey was, to be prepared better for the next outing.

Chapter Eight
THE SHADOW OF DOUBT

If a man will begin with certainties,
he shall end in doubts;
but if he will be content to begin with doubts
he shall end in certainties.

Sir Francis Bacon 1561-1626
English philosopher and essayist

Concerns

Before now, dear reader, you may not have realised that your challenge in the writing task is immense. Each assignment unfolds with uncertain character and an unfamiliar course. The certainty of accomplishment through *Exact Writing* is an aspirational affair with many residual doubts there to be found. It would be foolhardy not to unearth and confront these, especially before the beginning of the next writing task. Seldom will performance be entirely as first envisaged and, without enlightenment about it, there is a danger of stumbling onward without a second thought.

> Why confront doubts at the outset? How are doubts
> about past performance to be unearthed?

This short, concluding chapter looks at the merits of
Exact Writing, with particular reference to the handling
of doubts.

Attending to residual doubts is the servicing of your
vehicle of prose after a demanding journey to ensure that
it is 'fit for purpose' on its next outing; it is the carrying
out of an interim 'service schedule'.

Working with *Exact Writing*

Fundamentally, *Exact Writing* is a process that manages
doubt. It involves a complex, daunting performance
challenge that is the writing task. It applies to the written
work of professionally-minded people in which the
writer is striving for accuracy, precision and clarity by
responding to potential common intellectual and mood
faults. A resourceful thinking discipline, formed by a
conceptual model and aided by particular techniques,
empowers the writer to bring a Code of Responsibility,
backed by a Code of Awareness, into operation for
successful performance. In the face of many initial
doubts, through *Exact Writing* the writer successfully
reaches with some surety the goal destination of the
writing purpose, fully in accordance with a fundamental
performance aim.

Through *Exact Writing*, professionally-minded people

write less to convey more and to do so with influence. It requires dedicated effort in trying circumstances. Unhelpfully in an ever-busy world, there will have been many demands upon the writer's available time and undivided attention to the task in hand. Be that as it may, readers are likely to be in a similar situation. Readers are disinterested in the plight of the writer but, in contrast, the writer has an inescapable interest in the plight of the reader (Chapter Three ~ see *Communication Requirements*). No allowances will be made by readers for poor writing performance.

That state of affairs is compounded by the passage of time – days, weeks or months – between when the work is written in difficult, passing circumstances, and when it is most likely to be read in other circumstances by those who matter most. It is incumbent upon the writer, therefore, to embrace doubt about what has been accomplished, to appraise any evidence of a faltering advance along the *Exact Writing* way. A look at past performance in the cold light of day, when passing circumstances no longer press for attention, heralds the beginning of the next writing journey.

This type of focus is about pinpointing residual doubts about how well all important elements are conveyed, whether short cuts and shortcomings have become palpable. The performance indicators demand fluency and positive purposefulness when conducting the writing journey. In its finish, the writer may have faltered in those respects owing to depleted effort, the consequence of prevailing circumstances.

When looking at the effort in the workplace, never confuse activity with productivity. There is a universally experienced 80/20 principle that tells us that the minority of effort (say 20% or thereabouts) achieves the majority (say 80% or thereabouts) of results. What this shows is the failure to concentrate effort on what is important (80% of effort is misused for just 20% of results). This is due, most probably, to various prevailing circumstances.

Successful accomplishment of the writing task in hand should never become a casualty of competing time pressures from other demands, for the reasons fully set out throughout this book. A detached, unflustered look at the standard of the last written product will stimulate the writer's determination to combat wasted effort for greater productivity.

Productivity requires selectivity. Taking stock of what has happened sheds light on what other demands might usefully have been side-lined.

The dedicated effort that *Exact Writing* requires is there to be had, if only the writer were to concentrate on important elements. By dispensing with wasted effort on other things, there is ample potential not to suffer the consequences of unhelpful prevailing circumstances, which is the ultimate sophistication of accomplishment.

The practice of 'masterful inaction' is one way of seeking to do that in the future. Informed by past experience, it involves sound judgement of what other demands the writer may actively ignore, until such time as their importance is firmly established, which is usually by repeated requests of growing urgency. It is remarkable that issues arising from so many matters presented as important have a habit of taking care of themselves when left alone. With masterful inaction, the writer must also establish within the writing task itself what is worth letting go of and what is not. It is a question of staying focussed on work effort that matters most to keep the written product in good shape.

The shape of the written product is the conclusion of a writing task journey of discovery, for many reasons (Chapter Six ~ see *Successful Performance: The Aim*). Taking stock also of the shape of the previously written product sheds light on the pivotal value of creative leaps of inspiration and especially on what circumstances gave rise to them. The writer becomes better placed to manage these circumstances in the future.

The practice of 'sleep-working' is very effective in giving an enlightened focus to the writing task, one that continually evolves in response to the unresolved doubts and difficulties encountered. This is the practice of capitalising on the value of the twilight state when intuitive insight occurs, for obtaining instinctual knowledge (Chapter Two ~ see *Judgement*) It allows the writer to see clearly what is needed and exactly what is required to be done, without time-consuming repeated linear reasoning and diversions.

The practice of sleep-working sees sleeping hours as a highly productive time and not as a black hole separate from our lives. The writer connects the daytime experience with the night-time experience by prioritising and carrying over thoughts about emergent doubts and difficulties just before sleep. A notepad at the bedside is helpful because answers come thick and fast in the slow waking hours. Even with short assignments completed within the day, the writer will benefit from an opportunity 'to sleep on it' before committing to the final written product.

Sleep-working brings creativity to the fore. Creativity irresistibly invites the writer to become much more interested in the work in question. This goes to the core of motivation, not least in the writing task.

Much of this book is crafted with an enlightened focus through creative intuition born out of sleep-working, giving shape to this author's experience.

Unearthing Doubts

Successful accomplishment of the writing journey involves continually striving to do better, one way or another. An improved, challenging performance is persistently sought by professional people (Chapter Two ~ see *Personality*). It should become second nature to begin the writing task with doubts about the standard of execution of the previous assignment(s). Informed by those residual doubts, the writer is well placed to do better next time, with a more certain outcome.

Never be too busy to give attention to doubts and look at your previous written product as if reading it for the first time, because readers' first impressions are lasting impressions. This is no easy task because your mind is conditioned to read what you intended to write and not what appears on the page. With the passage of time, it is possible to change the way you look at things, and those things you are looking at will change from what you previously saw. Pinpoint doubts by asking the right questions about the effects of drifting away from the fluency and positive purposefulness of the *Exact Writing* way through depleted effort. Probe the written product against those performance yardsticks with an array of practical questions along these lines:

- Is there a satisfying shape to the written product, or is it lopsided?
- What is said about the work in question?
- Is the best advice possible projected?
- Does the written product have transparency, with no undertones (undercurrents of feeling) or overtones (subtle implications)?
- Is the written product complete with all necessary information?
- Are all relevant perspectives taken in?
- Is the approach focussed or blinkered?
- Are important elements all plainly conveyed?
- Is there a lapse into personal expediency for dealing with these?
- Is there a lack of care for the work in question?
- Are readers at a loss through constructions (words and their arrangements) entirely of personal convenience?
- Has the scope for confusion, criticism, complaint or challenge been minimised?
- Does the written product make sense, with logical

sequencing leading to inescapable conclusions?
- Will readers get the message in one go?
- With more effort, what more could have been done to cut out or express better, more simply in fewer words, the content and substance for manageable brevity?

Finally,
- Have I successfully communicated or just got by, leaving the reader to search for what was intended?
- Do I still wish to be associated with the written product?

Working with *Exact Writing* is very much about ensuring under any circumstances the fulfilment of the 'unspoken contract' between the professional person and readers, for communication with awareness and responsibility.

Mind, Method, and Misadventure

You have held in your hands a book about you – the measure of your professionalism when misadventure takes hold against where you need to be in mind and method for accomplished writing. Therefore, do not treat it as a textbook or manual of writing instructions. It is designed as a handbook to help you grow in stature with mental acuity to become fully professionally minded and resourceful, drawing upon the instructive experience of another. *Professionalism on the Page* is your means for developing an awareness and responsibility to fashion improved performance by carrying accuracy, precision and clarity with you – with the way of *Exact Writing*.

Take care of your words, for they show who you are and what you represent. Hear the unspoken thought owned by those you encounter in professional life and by the many others you do not see: 'Show me your words and I will tell you the person you are'. Make words work for you, bringing them under control with disciplined thought, finding the best in yourself and seeing the good in others along the way. Approach any writing task as a seriously worthwhile venture for you and the readership both. May *Professionalism on the Page* direct you towards the Holy Grail of manageable brevity.

A Final Thought

In the words of Josh Billings (Henry Wheeler Shaw 1818-1885) the acclaimed American humour writer and lecturer, 'There is great power in words, if you don't hitch too many of them together'.

V. ACCOMPLISHMENT

SAFE TRANSIT

Exact Writing is accuracy, precision and clarity
through mental acuity as impelled by awareness and
responsibility. It is accomplished through disciplined
thought.

These final pages are intended for easy reference.
They show the Code of Awareness and the Code of
Responsibility in full, followed by the approach and
headline techniques that assist the writer in complying.
Part V to *Professionalism on the Page* summarises the whole
mechanics to Exact Writing, whereby the safe transit of
readers permits the writer successfully to reach the goal
destination of the writing task.

CODE OF AWARENESS
(of Chapters One, Two & Three)

Linguistic

- capacity – know the capacity of prose for confusion and criticism, ever-mindful of the value of practices and conventions that aid understanding, which bring it under control.
- force – be clear about the pragmatic motive to write and greatly respect the penetrating force of prose, on thought, action or feeling.
- versatility – be alert to the seductive versatility of prose for straying beyond the pragmatic through mistreatment, occasioning the risk of wayward results that frustrate or distort meaning.
- gravity – observe the gravity of the work in question and the need for impressive, commensurate best advice: accurate, precise and clear.
- tone – value the customary literary skill in Standard English for establishing a commanding tone to the written product.
- impact – understand the impact of the written product, directly or otherwise upon people's lives, realising their point of view.
- expression – be sure about the expression of personal intellect or mental character, in line with professional identity, that readers reasonably expect to be on show.
- recollection – appreciate what content readers are required to remember and how to assist them.

- contemplation – see contemplation as a prerequisite to a commitment to words, which inform thinking and vice versa in repeated cycles for their choice and arrangement.
- validation – beware the function of result validation, anticipating the risks of challenges, especially those due to the potentially damaging effects of time constraints.
- ease – distrust the ease of effort associated with much of the language of electronic communication, seeing the need to furnish equal attention on what to say and how to say it.
- licence – realise that the image arising from any electronic communication warrants restraint to at least that of an educated person with expertise, one in which such a person leaves aside the casual or conversational and novel usage of language.

Self

- conscientiousness – be purpose-driven with conscientiousness for mounting personal standards with relentless self-criticism, line by line and word by word.
- emotional intelligence – let emotional intelligence impart a confident, positive outlook for doing well and look always to strengthen self-belief.
- resilience – believe in the best possible outcomes from any given situation with a determination to learn from and overcome any setbacks.
- temporal knowledge – ensure that the requisite

temporal knowledge about the subject, field and work in question is on hand.

- critical thinking – be poised for critical thinking to be second nature to temporal knowledge, for accurate, authentic content.
- reasoning – be ready with reasoning to firmly connect thoughts with a balanced weighing up of content.
- practical intelligence – draw from a fund of practical intelligence to enlighten analysis, synthesis and evaluation.
- instinctual knowledge – capture the twilight state of mind to profit from instinctual knowledge through intuitive insights and creative leaps in reasoning, accommodated through back-reasoning.
- composure – apply composure with a self-assured, considered and collected approach.
- competence – engage competence with a clear understanding of the focus to bring to bear on the 'what' and 'how' of the demands of the subject.
- honesty – stick to professional ethics (rights and wrongs) at every juncture, for honest endeavour in all respects.
- integrity – harness a consistency of actions through firmly applied principles of unquestionable integrity.
- diligence – follow the client's best interests (in whatever form and direction the brief takes) with diligence so that the task is executed as well as it can be, with nothing overlooked.

- objectivity – present objectivity fully, in line with dispassionate, impartial conduct.
- authority – communicate positional or other authority for maximum influence.
- courtesy – show courtesy to readers, especially in the interests of negating potential hostility towards the written product.
- legitimacy – use customary literary skill to reinforce the legitimacy behind what is expected of readers.

Task

- presence – bridge the communication gap through creating a writer-presence to readers and feel their presence continually, so not to write in isolation.
- handling – give guidance to meaning as much as possible when writing, especially for it to continue as long as possible when in the readers' hands, to attune readers appropriately.
- causation – meticulously establish and monitor the causation for the work in question, to verify the scope and detailed tasks.
- temperament – research temperaments to anticipate the relevance to readers of the work in question.
- alignment – seek an alignment with a light touch to leave no readers feeling excluded and write for the 'losing party' (those most hostile).
- inclination – arrange text to suit the inclination of candidate readers, concerning their preferred reading methods.
- strategy – respond especially to the strategy of

reading that is most appropriate to the content.

- concentration – structure the written product to aid concentration, particularly in the face of the potential blockages to quick understanding they are likely to encounter.
- urgency – make the reading experience trouble-free, swift and pleasant in deference to the urgency the reader brings to the written product.
- reference – go beyond the forensic treatment of readership and be a worthy ambassador for the profession, to meet and surpass the reference position for generally expected standards; see it as a threshold to be crossed.

CODE OF RESPONSIBILITY
(of Chapters Four & Five)

Intellectual

Weaknesses – *Inefficient Fluency*

- muddled through disorder by the messy writer – have a mental picture of the 'story' to tell for a clear focus (recollection), reflecting on the gist of the text as it unfolds, before finally setting it down and judiciously closing off peripheral matters (contemplation and handling). This is the practice of <u>unfolding the message</u>.
- vague through discord by the lazy writer – choose words and their arrangement consistently, correctly and wisely in the face of the potential for confusion and criticism, using them astutely at all times for aiding reading habits (inclination and strategy). This is the practice of <u>rationalising meaning</u>.
- elaborate through ostentation by the self-indulgent writer – see and hear words and their arrangement through the reader's 'eye-voice', as a novelist would, not through the 'thought voice' of the writer's speech (concentration), respecting the investment in the written product of precious reading time that is not to be wasted (urgency). This is the practice of <u>envisaging text</u>.
- overloaded through voracity by the extravagant writer – spot extravagances that are unhelpful to the simplicity of 'need to know' information fully in tune with readers' interests (temperament),

realising that readers will be thankful immediately to be able to seize upon what matters to them, free of needless elaboration (alignment). This is the practice of <u>streamlining content</u>.

- blurred through escalation by the guarded writer – stand confidently behind disappointing results (practical intelligence), resisting the natural temptation to bolster things with spurious or unnecessary content (integrity), mindful always of the need to narrow the communication gap between writer and reader (presence). This is the practice of frankly <u>upholding bare results</u>.

Failings – *Ineffective Fluency*

- inferior through laxity by the irresolute writer – intend always to be set apart from everyday average abilities, showing literary skill devoid of casual prose (ease, licence and tone), articulating the customary traditional stature of a professional person (authority and legitimacy) and providing a worthy standard (reference), befitting both intellect and professional identity (expression). Write deferentially to impress the reader, making words and their arrangement attractive, meaningful, manageable and relevant (courtesy). This is the practice of <u>showcasing stature</u>.

- misleading through distortion by the meddlesome writer – make any clarifications to inputs with great care and consistency (versatility), refraining from needless and misguided amendments (competence) for faithful influential content (force). This is the practice of <u>manifesting facts</u> ('hard' and 'soft', including the intellectual property of others).

That said, there are occasions for challenging inputs (next).

- unsound through incongruity by the neglectful writer – probe and investigate the face value of inputs (critical thinking), dealing with the insubstantial or contradictory ones, dismissing any that do not cross the respective factual or probability thresholds and organising all survivors by the weight they carry (validation). This is the practice of <u>testing knowledge</u>.

- fragile through incoherence by the reckless writer – leave no gaps in reasoning, exploring parallel lines of argument in response, engaging in further research for better temporal knowledge, and translating any disruptions into 'bridging assumptions', aided by instinctual knowledge, for checking with back-reasoning. This is the practice of <u>advancing the case</u>.

- unstable through misconstruction by the careless writer – keep the start-finish ends to the writing task in plain view and under review at all times, taking periodic and routine visits back to the start, developing or revising issues and objects (causation) and expressing them unequivocally through progressive refinement, for accurate thinking and where that leads (diligence). This is the practice of moderating context.

Motivational

Positive Purposefulness

- uneven through partiality by the reserved writer –
  stay professional in all respects and let no excuses
  dictate otherwise (conscientiousness). Separate
  the problem from the person. Study obstacles and
  hindrances from all angles to get at what lies past
  these. Be definitive and forceful about the minimum
  acceptable levels of such material for the task in
  hand, for the written product to satisfy expectations
  and scrutiny (honesty). This is the practice of
  <u>tackling impediments</u>.

- seductive through fixation by the insecure writer
  – make an effort to see above and beyond the
  parapet to the comfort zone of the familiar. Ask
  the right questions always and do not imagine or
  pretend to know the right answers. Expect and
  be prepared boldly to fail and quit graciously the
  lines of investigation and argument that become
  unproductive, in the interests of establishing the
  true and best result. Let the questions direct the
  quest, in deference to what readers need and
  expect (gravity and impact). This is the practice of
  <u>discovering substance</u>.

- impenetrable through distraction by the deceitful
  writer – use the negative forces behind aversion to
  activity and involvement as a source of information
  and feedback for self-knowledge and improvement,
  to become self-assured with a considered and
  collected manner (composure). Never doubt that

the written product will come to be scrutinised at some point when readers and peers will penetrate its cloak of jargon and see its impotent core for what it is. See the importance of the contribution the written product, however small, will make to one's personal professional stature and the standing of the profession, aiming always to prove capable (emotional intelligence). Know what is required and do it earnestly, compelled by having a firm approach in mind with clear, unavoidable steps to muster content (resilience). This is the practice of <u>activating potency</u>.

- poised through prevarication by the overcautious writer – refrain from giving equal weight and attention to unequal matters to please everybody. In other words, avoid 'sitting on the fence', such as with '...on the one hand X, but on the other Y...'. Come off the fence by getting to grips as far as possible with root causes. Subject neutrality is not dispassionate impartiality (objectivity). Rigorously distinguish between matters for inescapable conclusions. This is the practice of <u>championing positive results</u>.

COMPLIANCE WITH THE CODES
(of Chapters Six, Seven & Eight)

Aim (Chapter Six)
Write to convey best advice with influence. Aim to reach the goal destination of that writing purpose in the form *that readers trust the message in the written product, readily grasping it without reservations or doubt.* It means conducting the writing journey by carrying out the writing task as well as possible, with accuracy, precision and clarity, averting the potential for misadventure.

Method (Chapter Six)
Advance the writing task as a process of performance along the particular route of the writing journey unravelled by a conceptual model, VIP-FEAR. Think operationally with due deference to content and substance in these terms:

- vicariously – put readers centrally in mind as present and looking critically on.
- iteratively – sense to look back when writing forward on the page, keeping sight of the writing purpose, especially the start and finish ends of the writing journey.
- proportionately – focus unrelentingly on the way ahead, entertaining minor departures only, allowing others exceptionally but not beyond their worth, so that readers understand that all is heading for the same destination.

- fearsomely – see the requirements of the subject matter in a simple, methodical way that serves as writing stages (features, effects, analysis, results) for ensuring substantive content, particularly through the pre-empting of reluctance and risk aversion from fears.

Mentally chart the route of the writing journey to drive fluently and steer with positive purposefulness towards the goal destination with surety.

Firstly, thinking *vicariously* triggers these intents to responsible practices:

- unfolding the message – portraying substance graphically in line with what readers will follow to absorb.
- rationalising meaning – using the weight words carry to readers.
- envisaging text – choosing and arranging words for the 'eye-voice' of readers.
- streamlining content – seeing through a reader 'need to know' focus.
- upholding bare results – levelling a decisive uncomplicatedness that counts for a lot in readers' eyes.
- showcasing stature – seeing through readers' eyes, looking for a customarily distinctive written product.
- manifesting facts – acting as a reader looking on

in scrutiny, to be satisfied that the reporting of material facts throughout is true to their original meaning, especially when interpreting diverse 'soft' information so not to cause gratuitous controversy or offence.

championing positive results – gauging how the written product is to serve readers in the subject work area, so to be as forceful as possible, one way or another, about it.

Secondly, thinking *iteratively* triggers these intents to responsible practices:

- unfolding the message – establishing a 'story' by pausing as it unfolds to re-evaluate and retrospectively fit and refit the component parts, for a unified whole devoid of peripheral or divergent content.
- rationalising meaning – revisiting related words and expressions continually for potential amendment before setting down others with certitude.
- testing knowledge – making repeated backward qualifications or corrections to the source material together with subordinate amendments.
- advancing the case – looking back to go forward, taking in other lines of argument and/or bridging assumptions in order to summon supporting material.
- moderating context – undertaking backward checks by reviewing the starting position progressively to

where it has led, applying necessary adjustments throughout, to avert a lost finish or an unsatisfactory closing to the written product.

- tackling impediments – taking steps backwards to see the bigger picture, for repeated attempts by other means to get past hold-ups in problem areas.
- discovering substance – going forward experimentally in an open-minded, trial and error way for expansion and fitting coverage of the subject working dealing.

Thirdly, thinking *proportionately* triggers these intents to responsible practices:

- unfolding the message – rejecting immaterial content to keep focused upon substantive and determinative matters only.
- envisaging text – keeping to knowledge-appropriate language and meaningful words and expressions, strictly in line with the substance they are to reflect.
- streamlining content – refraining from unnecessarily sharing personal knowledge or other additional material, to exclude insignificant but overwhelming text.
- upholding bare results – resisting a 'smokescreen' of fortification in favour of straightforward, uncomplicated coverage of what has come about.
- testing knowledge – establishing the weight that source material should carry, especially where it is abundant or contradictory.

moderating context – abandoning lines of argument that do not relate to or recover the starting position.

activating potency – applying all of what must lie behind well-founded conclusions and results.

championing positive results – ceasing to hold all matters in equal measure, looking always to apportion weight to the most determinative ones, to forcefully deal with what counts most.

Finally, thinking *fearsomely* triggers these intents to responsible practices:

- unfolding the message – applying structure and logic.
- showcasing stature – allowing subject proficiency to show through in literary skill.
- manifesting facts – recognising the importance of source information to all that progressively follows.
- testing knowledge – looking for a sure foundation upon which to build subsequent analyses.
- advancing the case – finding that disconnection in subject analysis cannot be sustained and requiring commensurate accommodating analysis.
- moderating context – connecting ends to beginnings through a methodical course.
- tackling impediments – confronting difficulties with support from the uncontested demands of the recognised procedure.
- discovering substance – stretching beyond self-imposed boundaries, by sticking to imposed,

procedural demands.

- activating potency – responding to the lure of straightforward sequential steps through the subject matter.

Fluency (Chapter Seven)

Follow the VIP highway of FEAR approach industriously. Carry out the writing task with work effort suitably harnessed by fundamental, headline techniques as follows:

Efficient Fluency

- compaction – amplify meaning by stripping away wordiness, yielding best eye-voice images.
- thread – chart unifying thought(s), eradicating surprises or confusion.
- lucidity – show instantly recognisable true meaning, without recourse to context.

Effective Fluency

- thesis – provide a solid backbone of direction and course, from head to toe, connecting the start with its finish.
- directness – get straight to the point as quickly as possible.
- register – apply a trusted tone with impersonal yet lively expression, taking advantage of the 'weapons of influence'.

Positive Purposefulness

- thrust – inject an urgency with momentum from pace and contrast, showing commitment and

enthusiasm.
- resonance – get in tune with readers and never let confrontation or alienation take hold
- assimilation – absorb or suppress unhelpful moods with mood management before they do any harm.

Drive responsibly with a skilful effort to navigate with the writing task the route of the writing journey successfully.

Experience (Chapter Eight)

Fulfil under any circumstances the 'unspoken contract' between the professional person and readers for communication with awareness and responsibility. Welcome and exploit personal doubts about performance with practical questions along these lines:

- Is there a satisfying shape to the written product, or is it lopsided?
- What is said about the work in question?
- Is the best advice possible projected?
- Does the written product have transparency, with no undertones (undercurrents of feeling) or overtones (subtle implications)?
- Is the written product complete with all necessary information?
- Are all relevant perspectives taken in?
- Is the approach focussed or blinkered?
- Are important elements all plainly conveyed?
- Is there a lapse into personal expediency for dealing

with these?

- Is there a lack of care for the work in question?
- Are readers at a loss through constructions (words and their arrangements) entirely of personal convenience?
- Has the scope for confusion, criticism, complaint or challenge been minimised?
- Does the written product make sense, with logical, cohesive sequencing leading to inescapable conclusions?
- Will readers get the message in one go?
- With more effort, what more could have been done to cut out or express better, more simply in fewer words, the content and substance for manageable brevity?

Finally,

- Have I successfully communicated or just got by, leaving the reader to search for what was intended?
- Do I still wish to be associated with the written product?

REFERENCES

About Thinking

Coaching for Performance by John Whitmore. Nicholas Brealey Publishing. Fourth Edition 2009.

Critical Thinking Skills by Stella Cottrell. Palgrave Study Skills. Macmillan. Second Edition 2011.

Think Like a Freak by Steven D Levitt & Stephen J Dubner. Allen Lane Penguin Group. 2014.

Get Up and Grow by Philippa Davies. Hodder & Stoughton. 2001.

The Intuitive Way by Penney Peirce. Beyond Words Publishing (Grange Books). 2002.

Office Politics by Oliver James. Vermilion-Ebury Publishing, Random House Group. 2013.

About Writing

How to Write Essays & Assignments by Kathleen McMillan & Jonathan Weyers. Pearson. Second Edition 2011.

Professional Writing – The Complete Guide for Business, Industry and IT by Sky Marsen. Palgrave Study Guides. Second Edition 2007.

Write a Novel and Get it Published by Nigel Watts. Hodder Education 'Teach Yourself Series' 2010 edition.

Lost for Words by John Humphrys. Hodder & Stoughton. 2004.

Writing Space by Jay David Bolter. Lawrence Erlbaum Associates. 1991.

About English

Doing English by Robert Eaglestone. Routledge, Taylor & Francis Group. Third Edition 2009.

A Little Book of Language by David Crystal. Yale University Press. 2011.

The Complete Plain Words by Sir Ernest Gowers. Penguin Books. Third Edition 1987.

Strictly English by Simon Heffer. Windmill Books, Random House Group. 2011.

The Joy of English by Jesse Karjalainen. How To Books. 2012.

Rediscover Grammar by David Crystal. Longman. Revised Edition. 2003.